Snowdrop and
Tulip Yearbook
2020

An annual for amateurs and specialists
growing and showing
daffodils, snowdrops and tulips

in association with the Royal Horticultural Society, London

Editorial Board

Published in 2020 by
Royal Horticultural Society
80 Vincent Square
London SW1P 2PE

ISBN 9781911666097
© Royal Horticultural Society 2020
Opinions expressed by the authors
are not necessarily those of the
Royal Horticultural Society

Printed by Page Bros Group,
Norwich

Production Editor
Marina Jordan-Rugg

Correction

On page 31-33 of the 2019 Yearbook
we published Honouring Peter Barr
by Sally Kingston. Page 32 of the
article was a poem about Peter Barr
called Praise be to the daffodil king
that was written by John Byre. In the
third line of the left hand column
'there' should be on the next line. We
apologise to the author as this error
spoilt the rhyming scheme in the
opening verse.

Contents

Treat yourself to

The Plant Review

Where can plants take you?

Travel the globe from your armchair and make your interest an expertise
with the world's best plant magazine

Subscribe now at rhs.org.uk/theplantreview

Or send a cheque to: The Plant Review, RHS Membership
Subscriptions, PO Box 313, London SW1P 9YR

(payable to The Royal Horticultural Society)

Editorial

(Photo: Michael Baxter)

Well, what a year! Far easier on our bulbous beauties than on our human hearts. I hope this publication brings a little joy to what has been a difficult time for all.

I am thrilled to have taken on the position of Editor for this Yearbook and find myself *in situ* due to my love of daffodils. Trained at Pershore College and working in horticultural television, I am Editor of The Daffodil Society and honoured to have *Narcissus* 'Camilla Clara Kate' (pictured right) named after me, bred by the talented Brian Duncan.

In taking on this role I have huge shoes to fill, as we say goodbye to Malcolm Bradbury who has retired as Editor, having held the position since 1993. Malcolm has steered the ship superbly during this time, increasing tulip content and adding snowdrops in 2002, to what was originally solely a daffodil publication. I know you will join me in thanking him greatly for all his hard work.

Over the following pages, we have much to inform and entertain. I am particularly proud of our global survey of daffodil hybridising – a chance to hear from experts around the world. The weather may be dreary but we have plenty of information for filling your days with winter-flowering *Narcissus* cheer and, despite travel being far from our minds, we take you on a trip to Southern Spain. Back on UK soil, we hear how the RHS has been celebrating the 250th anniversary of the birth of that daffodil devotee – William Wordsworth – and catch up with a couple of valuable Plant Heritage daffodil collections. We also update you on the latest concerning the *Narcissus* monograph project, investigate the 3W-O or R colourations and hear from a respected daffodil nonagenarian with a great story to tell!

Moving to snowdrops, we put the spotlight on a rare example with a fascinating history, examine the best of the Irish and celebrate new findings in Slovenia. We also report back on the plethora of snowdrop events where galanthophiles gathered prior to lockdown.

For the tulip lover, we dissect everything from popular cultivars to new species found in recent years, in addition to offering tips on showing and growing. Plus a visit to a festival full of floriferous splendour.

A number of prominent members of our bulb community are celebrated in this edition, including stalwart Jan Pennings who has retired as RHS Bulb Committee Chairman. Sadly we have had to say goodbye to some much-respected members too, and our thoughts are with their families and friends.

Due to Covid-19, many shows did not take place this year; however for those that did, we are pleased to report back and congratulate the winning exhibitors and blooms.

I would like to thank Malcolm for his support and also James Akers, who has worked tirelessly on the organisation of photographs for this Yearbook. Thanks too must go to John Page for his tulip expertise, Reg Nicholl, John Gibson and the publication's Editorial Board.

I am certain that the flowering bulbs of 2021 will be anticipated and welcomed with exceptional enthusiasm.

Camilla Bassett-Smith

Exploring daffodils in S. Spain

Sally Kington

Narcissus papyraceus south of Montecorto, Málaga, begs the question of its difference from *N. panizzianus* (*photo* **C van der Veek**)

A band of daffodil explorers from Northern Ireland, England, the Netherlands, Latvia and Chile, led by the redoubtable Brian Duncan, converged on Málaga, southern Spain on 7 February 2020. We were between flower shows, or taking a rare breather from tight work schedules, or finding time before the start of an academic term in one hemisphere or spring flower production in another.

We zigzagged from Málaga to Madrid: first west to Ronda, then north-east by Benamejí and Cabra to Andújar and the Guadalquivir river before going higher up among the river's tributaries to Santa Elena. We then doubled back over a string of sierras to Almadén before descending to Puebla de Don Rodrigo and the path of the huge River Guadiana; then east again via Piedrabuena to motorway and city.

We have made forays into southern Spain before, Brian many times, and the level of satisfaction remains high. It is in the planning, then in spotting daffodils where expected and feeling smug, or spotting them off piste, unexpectedly, and feeling like stout Cortés on his peak in Darien. We meanwhile revel in the great sweep of the Spanish countryside, and this year in the lovely sunshine.

By our reckoning, we found ten species this

time, seven infraspecific taxa and seven hybrids. As we went from place to place, we pondered current opinion on classification and nomenclature, and the following sites are some that gave us particular food for thought.

Benamejí, Grazalema and Montecorto

A regular player in the natural daffodil show we were attending was *Narcissus fernandesii*, a variable species by all accounts but generally with two or more yellow flowers on a stem, separated and slightly reflexed petals, crenate corona, and (a useful clue to its identity devised by FJ Fernández Casas)[1] tube just slightly curved downwards to differentiate it from others in section Jonquilla: *N. gaditanus* (strongly curved down) and *N. jonquilla* (straight or slightly curved up).

Near Benameji, by a stalwart 16th-century bridge over the River Genil, is the site where a variant of *N. fernandesii*, identified by Fernández Casas as a separate species (later as a variety),[2] was named *cordubensis* in honour of its home province of Córdoba. This was bigger and more robust than the type and held 2-6 flowers on a stem.

In the course of time, however, certain daffodils from section Jonquilla were taken to be Fernández Casas's *cordubensis* in other parts of the country, notably near Grazalema in the province of Cádiz west of Ronda, and their distinctively lobed corona became, for some people, an identifier of the species. When, therefore, JF Ureña published the name *cerrolazae* for a population of the same daffodils from nearby Montecorto,[3] the feeling was that he had produced a synonym.[4] However, strong moves are being made now to retain *cerrolazae* for the daffodils with the lobed corona, which is thought to be a variety of *N. jonquilla*, and ensure that *cordubensis* stays with the plant from Benameji that has a simply crenate corona like *fernandesii*.

We went to all three sites, where *N. cordubensis* at Benamejí was in thin grass on steeply sloping, rock-strewn land under pine trees; *N. cerrolazae* at Montecorto in richer,

**Narcissus jonquilla subsp. cerrolazae
close to its type site south of Montecorto, Málaga**
(*photo* **J A Varas**)

more meadowy grass on gentler slopes; and the daffodils south of Grazalema that resemble those at Montecorto clustering on the grassy banks of a roadside ditch.

The Atajate road

Not far south of Ronda, on a giant rock face towering above the Atajate road, daffodils burst from every ledge and crevice. Among them was *N. fernandesii* with *N. assoanus*, another regular on our journey, also in section Jonquilla, stems usually topped by single or paired bright yellow flowers on slender tubes that lift them up to look at you. These two contend for parentage of an attractive hybrid for which this is the type site. *Narcissus × koshinomurae* has an inflorescence of up to four broad-petalled flowers in varying tones, the newly opening ones, at the bottom, yellow of petal and corona; the day-old ones ivory white of petal but often holding on to pale yellow in the wavy-edged, cup-shaped corona.

Fernández Casas named the hybrid in 1996,[5] estimating the parents to be jonquil daffodil *N. fernandesii* and a pure white tazetta on site that he considered to be *N. panizzianus*; the next year John Blanchard unwittingly named the same hybrid at nearly the same site *christopheri*, but he considered the jonquil parent to be *N. assoanus*.[6] The earlier name prevailed, taking precedence in accordance with the International Code of Botanical Nomenclature and making *christopheri* a synonym.[7] Meanwhile the jonquil parent is still not entirely settled in people's minds, though nuclear DNA results support *assoanus*.[8]

When John Blanchard first saw the hybrid at this site, it was tantalisingly out of reach and he was not, he said, prepared to sacrifice life or limb to get near enough for a close inspection. Fortunately for us, a fearless member of our group was game to climb right up high to inspect a stem and retrieve one too.

We had seen a white tazetta two days before, close to Málaga, in grassy glades in a birch wood, where in the past John Blanchard had told us it was probably not *N. papyraceus* but *N. panizzianus*. The main differences between the two, he wrote in his monograph in 1990,[9] were that *N. panizzianus* had smaller flowers than *N. papyraceus* and narrower leaves. When identifying the tazetta parent

of the hybrid on the Atajate road as *N. panizzianus*, he described it as 'a small form' of *N. papyraceus*.[10] Our smooth passage through these differences was rocked however by finding a wide range of flower diameter and leaf width on the Atajate road. Were the smaller specimens *panizzianus* and the larger *papyraceus*? Were they both on site? Or was it just the one of them, though varying in size according to the level at which it sprang from the cliff face? Another awkwardness, noted later, was that comparative measurements given by Abilio Fernandes in his seminal keys to the genus in 1968[11] put ours, of the birch wood flowers as well as of some on the Atajate road, outside his *panizzianus* bracket and into *papyraceus*. It would be good to travel round solely recording these two white tazettas, building up a picture of relative size and morphology from site to site. There is very little difference between the average DNA count of material passed to BJM Zonneveld (2008) as *N. papyraceus*, 33.825, and that of material identified as *N. panizzianus*, 33.525.[12]

ABOVE: *Narcissus fernandesii* north of Cabra, Granada (*photo* **J Ruksans**)
LEFT: *Narcissus × koshinomurae* on the Atajate road south of Ronda, Málaga, the lower flowers on a stem opening yellow, the upper ones fading to white (*photo* **JA Varas**)

ABOVE: West of San Lorenzo de Calatrava, Ciudad Real, parent *Narcissus cantabricus,* parent with *N. triandrus subsp. pallidulus* of the hybrid once called *N. × susannae* but now *N. × litigiosus*
LEFT: North of Santa Elena, Jaén *Narcissus × montielanus* with parents *N. luteolentus* (left) and *N. triandrus subsp. pallidulus* (right)
(*photos* S Kington)

Cabra

We saw daffodils with the same quirky colouring as *N. × koshinomurae* at Cabra in the province of Granada, where again *N. fernandesii* and *N. assoanus* were flourishing as well as *N. papyraceus*. They much resembled those from the Atajate road. However, following recent work here, Javier López-Tirado concludes that on this site such chameleon-like plants are a subspecies of *N. × koshinomurae*, or × *christopheri* as he calls it, which he has named *sanchezii*.[13]

The site is rich in species and hybrids and we were absorbed in trying to sort them out, but subspecies of hybrids become difficult to follow. However, another *fernandesii* hybrid, all yellow, thought by López-Tirado to be with *N. jonquilla*, was one we did think we had found. This he has named *N. × egabrensis*, from Cabra's Visigothic name Egabro.

Santa Elena and beyond

Handsome pure white hybrid *N. × montielanus* flanked the hairpin bends on a road outside Santa Elena that climbs east from the Despeñaperros gorge. Its parents, delicately pale if not quite white, were there too: *pallidulus*, whose classification as a subspecies of *N. triandrus* has not been much disputed since published in 1964; and *luteolentus*, a taxon in section Bulbocodium originally published as a subspecies of *N. cantabricus*,

recently considered to be that of *N. hedraeanthus*, but more recent molecular analysis shows it to be a likely hybrid between the two. The ranking of its bulbocodium parent matters to *N. × montielanus*, for its own taxonomic position shifts accordingly. I like the idea of the last outcome, where *montielanus* would be the accepted name, for the first two lead instead to synonymy, either with *N. × litigiosus* or with *N. × cazorlanus*.

There was plenty more of what the RHS treats as *N. cantabricus* subsp. *luteolentus* as we set off north-west from Santa Elena, and a particularly good site for *N. cantabricus* itself, that whitest of all members of section Bulbocodium. We were going west from San Lorenzo de Calatrava through the province of Ciudad Real, and from the road above a very deep-down river, we could see the brilliant lace of white flowers on a high, precipitously steep incline on the far side. Fortunately the road ran down to a bridge, and the site could be taken from the rear.

A hybrid, apparently between *N. cantabricus* and *N. triandrus*, called to mind the name *susannae*, the name *litigiosus* and certain intricacies of nomenclature. Fernández Casas published the name *N. × susannae* in 1980 for hybrids of *N. cantabricus* and *N. pallidulus* Graells (*N. triandrus* subsp. *pallidulus* of the RHS). The name *litigiosus*, first published by M del Amo y Mora in 1861, was determined by

9

Fernández Casas in 2005 to be that for hybrids of *N. cantabricus* and *N. concolor* (Haworth) Link (*N. triandrus* subsp. *triandrus* var. *concolor* of the RHS). However, as he considered at the time that *concolor* was the correct name for *pallidulus*, he noted that *N. × litigiosus* was conceptually the same as *N. × susannae* and that the earlier name *litigiosus* took precedence over the later *susannae*. Whatever you call them, hybrids of *N. cantabricus* and *N. triandrus* subsp. *pallidulus* are most attractive: pure white pendent flowers with shapely airily swept back petals and cup-shape corona lightly fluted.

Puebla de Don Rodrigo

Two more *Narcissus triandrus* hybrids occupy the environs of Puebla de Don Rodrigo, a town in the province of Ciudad Real near the end of our journey. These and their respective second parents, *N. bulbocodium* and *N. rupicola*, bear witness to the amount of variation to be found in the genus *Narcissus*. After spending 20 years as registrar of cultivated daffodils, which are clones, I am particularly taken by this aspect of the wild ones: frequent variability of self-pollinated seedlings and multiplication of variation by intraspecific hybridisation.

The road east out of Puebla de Don Rodrigo runs between the River Guadiana on one side

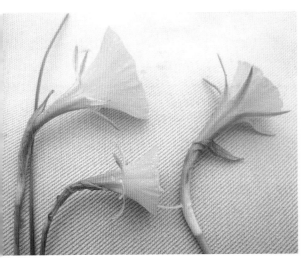

and pine woods and rocky outcrops rising away from the other, where *N. bulbocodium* appears. We had left white *N. cantabricus* behind; now there was nothing but golden-yellow *N. bulbocodium*. And it came not only in different sizes, but also with variable intensity and extent of green in tube and perianth, and with the corona, which is on the whole obconical, sometimes proportionately short, sometimes long. *Narcissus rupicola* was here as well, also variable: the corona sometimes spread open, shallow and wavy-edged, sometimes deeper and like a little bowl, sometimes with higher and straighter sides.

The breadth of variation in *N. bulbocodium* subsp. *bulbocodium* leads to 'lumping' and 'splitting'. For example, it is described as large and showy in Haworth's *Corbularia conspicua* (1831),[15] was treated as *Narcissus conspicuus* by D Don (1838),[16] was accepted by John Blanchard (1990) as the name for all 'strong growing yellow European bulbocodiums',[17] but some recent accounts lump it into *N. bulbocodium* subsp. *bulbocodium*.[18]

As for splitting, one more heavily striped specimen among our finds, in a darker green than most, echoed something I was reading up on our return: a possible descendant from Haworth's *Corbularia gigas* ('the giant')[19] that Abílio Fernandes named *N. bulbocodium* subsp. *quintanilhae* in 1987[20] and that Fernández Casas well and truly split from *bulbocodium* by raising it to species level in 2005.[21] In fact BJM Zonneveld confirmed its difference from *N. bulbocodium* (2008), putting its chromosome count at 21 or even 42 compared with 14 for the type. But as to any connection with our specimen, probably not. It is described with the tube striped green and the green running up the back of the petals, but tube, petals and corona are underlyingly pale yellow, rarely golden yellow like ours.

The road going over the river and north-

***N. bulbocodium* east of Puebla de Don Rodrigo, Ciudad Real province, variable in size and in density of green on tube and petals** (*photo* **S Kington**)

east out of town climbs up to dryer, higher land. Here wide expanses of *N. bulbocodium* were in the grass among rocks and scrub on shallow slopes up from the road; *N. rupicola* was on a rocky bluff. *Narcissus triandrus* subsp. *pallidulus* intermingled, producing *N. × fosteri*, the hybrid with *N. bulbocodium*, and *N. × rupidulus* that with *N. rupicola*, the ones we found having particularly fetching permutations of characters passed down from their respective parents: *N. × fosteri* yellow and upward-facing like *N. bulbocodium*, with the long reflexed petals and prettily cup-shaped corona of *N. triandrus*, and bright orange anthers from who knows where; *N. × rupidulus* yellow like *N. rupicola*, but with narrow reflexed petals like *N. triandrus* and gracefully bent head.

Neither do hybrids escape the splitters.

The amount of variation among offspring of one set of parents is corralled by the fact that all are given the same hybrid name. The slippery slope is when infraspecific names are given to variations of those offspring, even though each is probably sterile and hardly likely to be seen again or, if by chance fertile, packed with variability and far from easy to circumscribe.

This intriguing trip ended on a distinct high note among such variants and hybrids. The mist did come down on our last day, but was greeted with pleasure when the dimmer light made for better photography.

Monograph

Since John Blanchard wrote a comprehensive and penetrating account in 1990 of *Narcissus* in the wild, a great deal of new work has been done, particularly by botanists on their home ground in Spain and Portugal: not only providing new insights into existing names and classifications but also identifying and describing numerous new species and hybrids. John's account is due for revision and expansion, and in this respect, Dr John David, Head of Horticultural Taxonomy at the Royal Horticultural Society, writes: A new edition of this authoritative work that has stood the test of time is long overdue. More details on plans to produce it are given in the report on the *Narcissus* Monograph project (see pp55–57).

ACKNOWLEDGEMENT

I am grateful to John David for the generous time he takes to help elucidate matters of classification and nomenclature.

Sally Kington *was formerly Secretary of the RHS Daffodil and Tulip Committee and International Daffodil Registrar*

Seen north of Puebla de Don Rodrigo was a particularly yellow form of *N. × fosteri*, the cross between *N. bulbocodium* and *N. triandrus* subsp. *pallidulus* (*photo* **J A Varas)**

REFERENCES

1. FJ Fernández Casas (1996) Narcissorum notulae, II. *Fontqueria* 44: 254

2. FJ Fernández Casas (1982) De flora occidentale. *Fontqueria* 1: 10

3. JF Ureña (1994) Nueva especie del género *Narcissus* L., sect. Jonquillae DC. de Ronda (Málaga). *Botanica Complutensis* 19: 83–88

4. JW Blanchard (1998) Narcissus update. *Alpine Garden Society Bulletin* 66 (3) 330

5. FJ Fernández Casas (1996) Narcissorum notulae, II. *Fontqueria* 44: 254–55

6. JW Blanchard (1997) *Narcissus* × *christopheri*: A newly described wild hybrid. *Daffodil and Tulip Yearbook* 1997–8: 10–11

7. NJ Turland et al (eds) (2018+ [continuously updated]) International Code of Nomenclature for algae, fungi, and plants (Shenzhen Code) adopted by the Nineteenth International Botanical Congress Shenzhen, China, July 2017: Article H.10.2, Note 2, Ex. 6 (https://doi.org/10.12705/Code.2018)

8. BJM Zonneveld (2008) The systematic value of nuclear DNA content for all species of *Narcissus* L. (*Amaryllidaceae*). *Plant Systematics and Evolution* 275 (1–2) 109–132

9. JW Blanchard (1990) *Narcissus*: a guide to wild daffodils. Alpine Garden Society, Woking

10. See reference 6 above

11. A Fernandes (1968) Keys to the identification of native and naturalized taxa of the genus *Narcissus* L. *Daffodil and Tulip Yearbook* 33: 56

12. See reference 8 above

13. J López-Tirado (2019) A natural laboratory in southern Spain: new hybrids of wild daffodils (*Narcissus, Amaryllidaceae*). *Phytotaxa* 394 (2) 161–170

14. FJ Fernández Casas (2005) Tres narcisos Granadinos descritos por Mariano del Amo y Mora. *Adumbrationes ad Summae Editionem* 12: 1–16. Also **FJ Fernández Casas (2005).** Narcissorum notulae, VI. *Fontqueria* 55: 271

15. AH Haworth (1831) A monograph on the subordo V of *Amaryllidaceae* containing the *Narcissineae*: 1. In Robert Sweet, *The British Flower Garden* 2nd series, 1

16. D Don (1838) *Narcissus conspicuus*. In Robert Sweet, *The British Flower Garden* 2nd series, 4: t.326

17. See reference 9 above

18. E Rico et al. (eds) (2013). *Flora Iberica* 20. Also WCSP (2020). World Checklist of Selected Plant Families. Facilitated by the Royal Botanic Gardens, Kew (http://wcsp.science.kew.org/)

19. See reference 15 above

20. A Fernandes (1987) Rôle de la triploïdie dans l'évolution chez *Narcissus* sect. Bulbocodii. *Boletim da Sociedade Broteriana* 2nd series 60: 305–306

21. FJ Fernández Casas (2005). Narcissorum notulae, VI. *Fontqueria* 55 (34) 269

RHS celebrates the 250th anniversary of William Wordsworth's birth

Jonathan Webster

Early-spring-flowering *Narcissus* **'February Gold' at RHS Garden Hyde Hall (***photo* **RHS/Joanna Kossak)**

Plants are the heart and soul of Royal Horticultural Society (RHS) gardens and we are always looking at our varied collections and seeking new ways to display and highlight our different plant groups within them, in order to delight and educate our visitors. Linking these to people in history and noted anniversaries is a great way to bring the collections alive and show the influence plants can make in our society.

This year marked the 250th anniversary of the birth of the William Wordsworth in 1770,

one of England's most famous romantic poets. Wordsworth became poet laureate in 1843, a role he held until his death in 1850. He is perhaps best remembered for his joyous poem *I Wandered Lonely as a Cloud*, commonly known as Daffodils, which expresses his delight in coming across a large drift of wild daffodils and also celebrates his affinity with nature and the beauty of the Lake District in which he lived. What better way for us than to mark this auspicious occasion with a sea of gold across the four RHS gardens this spring?

13

Drifts of *Narcissus* 'Sir Winston Churchill' at RHS Garden Harlow Carr (*photo* **RHS/Jason Ingram**)

All four gardens also staged a special outdoor exhibition, which featured, along with Wordsworth's story, interesting daffodil facts, DNA research by RHS scientists and the role of daffodils in art, culture and religion.

In spring, the RHS gardens awake with a riot of colour that is full of interest to all who visit. What would the garden be without bulbs? They create a real wow factor with seas of colour, adding almost instant drama to the landscape as the flowers emerge.

Each year we plant thousands more bulbs to extend the display, adding to existing groups in grass, meadows and borders. In addition, pots and bedding schemes change each year and can showcase new cultivars alongside old favourites with guaranteed performance.

RHS Garden Rosemoor

Each year at RHS Garden Rosemoor in Devon, we plant in excess of 40,000 bulbs. In autumn 2019, 12,000 of these were of 30 daffodil species and cultivars including early-flowering *Narcissus* 'February Gold' AGM and 'Rijnveld's Early Sensation' AGM, which flowers as early as December here; sweet-smelling 'Grand Soleil d'Or' and late-blooming 'Thalia'. 'Rosemoor Gold' was released in 2004 for the 200th anniversary of the RHS, and 2,000 more were planted in the Lady Anne's garden last autumn, where it is naturalising beautifully. We also hold a collection of cultivars bred at the Rosewarne Research Station in Cornwall from the 1950s to 1980s. When it closed they were taken to Wisley, but a few years ago the collection came back to the South-West.

RHS Garden Hyde Hall

RHS Garden Hyde Hall in Essex has a dramatic wide and open farming landscape with drifts of daffodils planted throughout. Swathes of daffodils line the approach to the garden, offering a cheerful greeting in the early months of the year. Elsewhere, they smother the bulb bank of the Queen Mother's Garden and are spring stars in the garden's Floral Fantasia display.

RHS Garden Harlow Carr

RHS Garden Harlow Carr in North Yorkshire took on a distinctly golden hue as a host of daffodils put on a show across the 23.2 hectare (58-acre) garden. More than 70 different daffodil cultivars provided up to eight weeks of colour, featuring favourites such as 'Jetfire' AGM, well known for its distinctive orange trumpet,'February Gold' (flowering from February through until March); and the all-time classic 'Tête-à-tête' AGM (Although originally published as 'Tête-à-Tête' this format of the name is contrary to Article 35.12 of the ICNCP and has to be written as given here).

RHS Garden Wisley

RHS Garden Wisley in Surrey has daffodils to delight everyone, with naturalised *Narcissus* species in the Alpine Meadow, to generous drifts in Seven Acres, Oakwood and the Jubilee Arboretum.

New plantings of daffodils were made in the Pinetum with some 35,000 bulbs planted last autumn, including 'February Gold', 'Jack Snipe' AGM and 'Jenny' AGM, creating a carpet of spring colour under the majestic pines. The Alpine Meadow becomes a sea of golden yellow from the delicate and distinctive flower heads of hoop petticoat daffodil, *N. bulbocodium* AGM.

Consequently, at the start of lockdown and during spring, all the RHS Gardens were awash with colourful daffodils, but their beauty will continue and more visitors will enjoy them in the years to come.

Jonathan Webster *is Curator of RHS Garden Rosemoor and has worked for the RHS for nearly 25 years, starting at RHS Garden Wisley.*

RHS Garden Rosemoor awash with its namesake ***N.* 'Rosemoor Gold'** (*photo* **RHS/Jason Ingram**)

Dainty *Narcissus* **'Jack Snipe' in the Pinetum at RHS Garden Wisley** (*photo* **RHS/Joanna Kossak**)

Two National Plant Collections of *Narcissus* cultivars

Malcolm Bradbury with Caroline G Thomson and Gary Firth

The seven National Plant Collections of *Narcissus* cultivars held by members of Plant Heritage vary considerably in size and enable the public to see themed selections of cultivars. This article looks at two very different collections. Caroline Thomson writes about the Backhouse Centre in Scotland, where 15,000 daffodils, mostly with Backhouse-bred cultivars in their pedigree, can be seen and Gary Firth describes the creation of a small collection of daffodils raised by the late Noel Burr and grown by members of the Plant Heritage Sussex Group. We plan to cover the remaining collections – focused respectively on commercial cultivars, daffodils raised before 1930 and cultivars raised by the Brodie of Brodie, Alec Gray and the Rev G H Engleheart – in a future edition.

Plant Heritage

The range of plants that we grow in our gardens changes continuously. Plants become fashionable or fall out of favour, diseases destroy previously vigorous commercial stocks and healthy plants are withdrawn from sale when more profitable alternatives become available. Consequently, although gardeners have an ongoing choice of newly introduced plants to buy, they also face a steady loss of many that are both distinctive and attractive. The danger, made worse by the continued loss of small nurseries and the focus of modern plant-marketing techniques on a narrower range of fast-selling products, is that gardeners are often unable to buy some plants that they want and genetic material that could be used for breeding new plants is lost.

In 1978 concerns about this plant loss led the RHS to hold a conference on 'The practical role of gardens in the conservation of rare and threatened plants', which in due course led to the creation of the National Council for the Conservation of Plants and Gardens (renamed Plant Heritage in 2009). Working through 31 local groups, members of Plant Heritage now have about 650 National Plant Collections caring for about 95,000 plant taxa.

The key points common to all National Plant Collections are that plants should be recorded, their provenance known and they must be available for the public to see.

● Details of how to see the seven National Plant Collections of *Narcissus* cultivars post Covid-19 can be found online at www.plantheritage.org.uk

Part of the Backhouse *Narcissus* National Plant Collection in cold frames at Backhouse Rossie, Kingdom of Fife (*photo* Backhouse Rossie)

The National Plant Collection of Backhouse *Narcissus* cultivars, the Kingdom of Fife

Caroline G Thomson, MA, Director of the Backhouse family's Heritage Centre and Curator of the Backhouse Heritage Daffodil Collection

Narcissus 'Lady G. Buchan-Hepburn' is named for the author's mother (*photo* **Backhouse Rossie**)

At our home, Backhouse Rossie, we grow daffodils hybridised by our ancestors over a 150-year period: William Backhouse (1807–1869), his sons Henry (1850–1936) and Robert Ormston (1854–1940), Robert's wife Sarah Dodgson (1857–1921) and their son William Ormston (1885–1962). My article in the 2016 Yearbook (pp18–24) examined their work in the genus *Narcissus* and our Backhouse Centre preservation work.

From the mid-1800s–1962 my Quaker forebears introduced 956 *Narcissus* cultivars, including three that formed the basis of many of today's popular daffodils. However, the *RHS Plant Finder* 2008 showed only 13 of these available in commerce. Consequently, time is spent researching, plant hunting with my husband and trialling cultivars to confirm their correct IDs in consultation with Dr David Willis. The text below details a recent research break, but highlights the fragility of *Narcissus* left to time.

One *Narcissus* cultivar was identified and confirmed as true, due to the discovery of a piece of paper at the Backhouse Centre with barely legible writing recording the words CJ Backhouse followed by a numbered code, believed to have been scribed by William himself. Further similar archive material was found and my analysis of these numbers led to a 'working' conclusion that these codes were William's personal shorthand.

This deciphering process revealed William's methodology in recording his hybrid crosses, planting locations, seedling descriptions and observations, which are now in a readable format. It was an exciting moment when (with permission) I followed William's deciphered number sequence from the tiny scrap of paper that led me to the exact spot in the seedling beds where William had planted this cultivar more than 140 years ago, named after his son Charles James Backhouse. It is hoped further cultivars can be identified from the deciphered records. However, despite some successes, a disheartening story has emerged of codes leading to marshy ground, areas of coarse grass or encroaching conifers, but I believe plans are under way to protect this fragile site.

The Backhouse Centre has a horticultural reference library (book donations gratefully received) and Backhouse family exhibition. Flourishing in the grounds is the Heritage Narcissus collection and descendants from key *Narcissus* cultivars such as 'Emperor', 'Empress' and 'Weardale Perfection'.

New registered cultivars were hybridised from our forebears' flowers – N. 'Backhouse Rossie Estate' 3W-YYO retains the charm of early hybrids and elegant N. 'Lady G. Buchan-Hepburn' 2Y-YYO (pictured) with a primrose-coloured perianth is named after my mother Georgina Elizabeth (1928–2020), a dedicated supporter of this project.

National Scientific status is being sought for the already-held National Heritage Plant Collection status for our Backhouse forebears' cultivars. See www.backhouserossie.co.uk for opening times and Scotland's Daffodil Festival.

N. 'Cherrygardens' (*photo* **Michael Baxter**)

Dispersed National Plant Collection of Noel Burr *Narcissus* cultivars

Gary Firth, Plant Heritage Collections Co-ordinator for Sussex

Noel Burr was a keen amateur breeder of daffodils, based near Mayfield in Sussex, who had bred and registered 58 cultivars and named many after Sussex villages such as Dallington, Danehill, Fletching and Ringer. He also operated a catalogue of surplus bulbs for sale, which saw many of his cultivars exported to places like New Zealand, Australia and the USA. In early 2017, I was approached by one of our Sussex Plant Heritage members concerned that he was in a poor state of health and that many of the cultivars he had registered might be lost to cultivation.

We didn't have the facilities to collect and grow all the cultivars that might be available, so I conceived the idea of a dispersed National Plant Collection, held by members of the Sussex Group of Plant Heritage.

In a dispersed collection, a number of individuals hold a single National Plant Collection dispersed across many different sites. It has many advantages, especially where a plant genus might be susceptible to plant diseases, cross-fertilisation or where there are space limitations for an individual grower.

Eight members offered to join the scheme and we were able to source a dozen or so cultivars from three of the major UK daffodil suppliers plus a specialist bulb auction. Plant

Heritage accepted our initial proposal to hold this as a dispersed National Plant Collection in December 2017 and 13 Sussex members are now involved. Roger Braithwaite of Bramcote Bulbs offered us a further nine cultivars bringing our total up to 19. Following a further two seasons of growth, an application for full dispersed National Plant Collection status was approved in the summer of 2019.

Our dispersed group of collection holders is now thriving. We have full photographic records of all cultivars, have started a herbarium collection, have learnt how to twin scale and one of our group has even started cross-pollinating some of the cultivars. 'Cherrygardens' 2W-GPP (pictured) is a fine cultivar, registered in 1978, which is still seen at many shows today along with several other cultivars in our current collection that have been shown and won prizes for our members at local shows in Sussex. My personal favourites are 'Fletching' 1W-W and the rather nice double-flowered 'Hever' 4Y-Y. Some of the later have now been transferred to the Head Gardener at Hever Castle to be twin scaled and grown on there.

Sadly Noel passed away in July 2017 (his obituary was published in the 2017 Yearbook, pp17–18), unaware that efforts were under way to save his unique contribution to the daffodil world. We continue to search for other Noel Burr cultivars before they become totally lost to cultivation and have high hopes that at least a few more will be found, including perhaps some of his last registered cultivars such as the quaintly named 'Piglet' 2O-R registered in 2006 and 'Buckhurst Park' 2W-O, 'Dundle' 3W-YOO, 'Molisher' 1W-W and 'Wessons' 2Y-Y00, all registered in 2007.

Malcolm Bradbury *is an amateur daffodil exhibitor, judge, hybridiser, writer, speaker and former long-running Editor of this publication.*

Living a life of hope

Reg Nicholl

My first encounter with daffodils took place some 80 years ago when our school geography teacher told of the wonderful display to be seen in the then-small north Lancashire town of Broughton-in-Furness, later to be transferred by Keith Joseph, into Cumbria.

Fired by her enthusiasm, a group of we lads sallied forth on our bikes, a journey of some 32km (20 miles), and were astonished by what we saw – fields of Wordsworthian daffodils. It was just a matter of picking a bunch, tying them to our handlebars and bringing them home in the ever-pouring rain.

The almost constant precipitation falling on my hometown of Barrow-in-Furness was such that the local joke was that the residents there had webbed feet and I resolved to move to drier parts.

Fast forward 25 years I moved 'south' and settled, although I was unaware at the time, to England's driest county, Essex. With a brand-new house, costing the princely sum of £3,750, came something I'd not previously owned, namely a garden. For assistance in knocking it into shape I joined the local horticultural society, and subsequently the Royal Horticultural Society.

Damascene moment

A couple of years later, I was asked to assist in the judging of a Spring Show in the neighbouring town of Elm Park. This then turned out to be my Damascene moment, not quite on a par with the chap who trod along the Syrian road, but to me enlightening. The Best Bloom award we decided was a superb division 2 flower, which didn't have a name but simply written on its ticket was Seedling No 5. I sought out the raiser, one Eddie Jarman, and fired by his enthusiasm I decided I would try and emulate him. The seedling 'Border Chief' × 'Majorca', incidentally, was later registered as 'Bojangle' 2Y-YYO.

Advised I would need something better than the likes of 'Texas' 4Y-OO growing in my garden, I turned to famed Irish breeder and grower Lionel Richardson, and purchased for what I thought were rather steep prices, 'Kingscourt' 1Y-Y, 'Bizerta' 2W-Y, 'Narvik' 2Y-O and 'Verona' 3W-W.

The following season, armed with the usual paraphernalia of brush, tweezers, string and labels, I collected my first seeds, planted them in square plastic butcher's liver pots, in John Innes compost No.2, and so began the long five-year wait. As the years progressed I carried out the same hopeful procedure, and at the same time purchased additional bulbs for breeding.

N. 'Saxby' (*photo* **Reg Nicholl**)

Where to plant all these seedlings was becoming a problem, but luckily I heard of an elderly couple who were struggling to maintain their allotment, which was just a few minutes from my home and so I transferred them there. This was a happy association for the next three years, abetted by the lady owner whose very strong tea tasted more like creosote than the national beverage. However, sadly within a few months of one another the pair passed on and I was given notice to quit.

Eddie Jarman, who lived some 32 km (20 miles) away, kindly offered me the end of his very long garden and I took up his offer, but the travelling at weekends was a tiresome business and I decided to find somewhere nearer home. I was reluctant to rent a Local Authority allotment as I had heard tales of constant pilfering but I had no option as I was now an expectant daffodil father. Back in Rainham I moved my daffodils into an allotment that was once a gravel extraction pit filled with soil from goodness knows where and this was where my eagerly anticipated first flowers bloomed. However, it was something of an anti-climax as the result was a mundane collection of rather nondescript flowers. Never mind next year must be better as the crossing of more selective flowers

N. **'Marion Pearce'** (*photo* **Michael Baxter**)

would prove. Not at this site I'm afraid because the local Council had been informed by the Henry Doubleday Research Association that the site was badly contaminated by cadmium, from men's toiletries apparently, as the result of sewage being dumped there and the top 61cm (2ft) would have to be removed and replaced.

Off then after digging up all the bulbs and transferring them to the alternative allotment site where I stayed for the next 40 years and, just to safeguard against possible expulsion, I took on the job of Site Steward.

First successes

I had showed my seedlings at local shows with a little success, mainly because there was negligible opposition, and decided to join the big boys at the RHS. I did manage to win a few cards and graduated from single blooms, to threes and eventually to a six and was given a piece of silver for the latter. I had no intention of naming them but Ron Scamp liked one and even registered it for me. 'Greenodd' 3W-YYW ('Easter Moon' × 'Cool Crystal') (pictured), named after a Lake District village, as eventually were 'Torver' 2Y-W ('Daydream' × 'Chiloquin') and 'Swarthmoor' 2YYW-Y ('Chiloquin' × 'Delectable').

Aged 60, I had been having medical problems but feeling fitter after a six-month layoff I visited my doctor, having advised my Chief Engineer I would be returning to work. However, she thought otherwise and insisted I took early retirement. Quite pleased at the outcome, I picked a bunch of one of my seedlings and took it to the surgery. The following day she rang, asked me to visit the surgery where I found a photographer who took a picture of her, me and the flowers. A few weeks later I was given a copy of the *British Medical Journal Newsletter* in which a picture of us and an article appeared! Thus 'Bismillah Awan' 2W-YYO ('Bizerta' × 'Tudor Minstrel') was named after her. Later, I gave her the whole stock of bulbs, as she was returning to Pakistan, which is something I would not recommend because only last year, shortly before his death, I had an email from noted Australian raiser Fred Silcock, asking if I could spare a bulb.

Trying for something different I crossed 'Delia' 6W-YWP with 'Raspberry Ring' 2W-GWP and was pleased with the outcome – 'Little Jazz' 6W-WRR, which has done quite well in the USA. Then a little and large combination – 'Perky' 6W-Y with 'King Size' 11aY-Y – resulted in a spiky-looking flower. There was only one name for it so I wrote to the great comedian and he was delighted to have a daffodil called after him – 'Spike Milligan' 11aY-Y.

Split-corona cultivars

When I first saw the Gerritsen split-corona cultivars many years ago I was certainly in the minority but nevertheless captivated by them. Choosing one of John Lea's great flowers, 'Achduart' 3Y-R, and crossing it with one of Gerritsen's best raisings, 'Congress' 11a Y-O, gave me four of my most pleasing flowers: 'Duke Ellington' 11aY-YYO, 'Jean Nicholl' 11aY-O, 'Saxby' 11aY-YYO (pictured) and 'Marion Pearce' 11aY-YYO (pictured).

Blooms of the last named were among the daffodils I transported in a cardboard box in the plane overhead locker, to the American Daffodil Society's 50th Anniversary Convention and National Daffodil Show in 2004 at Washington DC, where two of them won first prizes. Another of my flowers, the Clive Postles-raised 'Reg Nicholl' 2Y-YYR, was Best Intermediate in show.

'Marion Pearce' had also featured as a seedling, along with four other split-corona seedlings at their Convention way back in 1994 in Portland, Oregon, in the class for five 'splits' and given first, beating the leading American breeder, I immodestly say! Back home, more recently it was given Best Intermediate and Best Division 11 at the RHS Daffodil Show in 2015 when grown and shown by Richard Hilford.

The stock of 'Duke Ellington' was asked for,

and given to a newly formed bulb company, which unfortunately foundered after a year or two, while 'June Christy' 2W-P ('Broomhill' × 'Shell Bay'), my particular favourite, was introduced by Copford Bulbs. I'll put my trumpet away now.

The final two of the 13 named daffodils I've bred are 'Helen Nicholl' 2W-Y ('Berry Gorse' × 'Tudor Minstrel') and 'Beverley Nicholl' 2Y-Y ('Gold Mine' × 'Golden Aura'), people with whom I have a certain connection.

Growing on an allotment has its pluses as I mentioned earlier but also its drawbacks. For instance, one year my stock was infested with eelworm, which unfortunately, among others took the seedling 19/89 ('Sabine Hay' × 'Creag Dubh'), which I had exhibited at the RHS, and which, because of the good form and colour, I had high hopes for. Alas all I have is the colour transparency.

Now in my 92nd year I still eagerly look forward with great anticipation to what the new season may bring forth among my still un-flowered seedlings.

Reg Nicholl *is an Honorary Member of the RHS Bulb Committee, former President and Chairman of the Daffodil Society and an experienced exhibitor, judge and hybridiser of daffodils*

N. 'Greenodd' (*photo* Reg Nicholl)

Winter daffodils

John Gibson

A number of daffodils flower during the winter months of December, January and February, bringing much-needed joy to the beholder. The following interesting oddities are some of my favourites, which give me much pleasure through the winter.

Narcissus papyraceus

Paperwhite daffodils or *N. papyraceus*, to give them their correct botanical name, produce flowers periodically over the course of the winter period. The bulbs are widely available and provide an easy and economical introduction to winter flower daffodils.

Narcissus broussonettii

N. broussonettii is an interesting species found in western Morocco. The solitary member of its section Aurelia, it is generally regarded as an autumn-flowering species. However, as John Blanchard mentions in his book *Narcissus: A guide to wild daffodils* (AGS 1990), its flowering time in the wild stretches from September to January, thereby falling comfortably into the winter period. It usually flowers in December in cultivation, for me.

The foliage is robust and springs vigorously from the large Tazetta-like bulb. The pure white, pleasantly scented flowers are carried in umbels of three to seven florets, each having a long, slender tube. Visually it differs from *N. papyraceus* by lacking any corona; the golden stamens are distinctly biseriate: three inserted at the throat of the tube, with three below it.

Narcissus viridiflorus

N. viridiflorus is another autumn-flowering species that often waits until the winter period

before flowering; the timing appears to depend on when watering is commenced. I've found it a troublesome plant to consistently flower well and summer temperatures seem to affect initiation. On occasion it performs superbly and its powerful scent fills the greenhouse on a warm day, but in other years the flowers are sparse, with only single florets.

Narcissus cantabricus subsp. *cantabricus* var. *kesticus*

Many members of the Bulbocodium section start to show leaf growth very rapidly after the compost becomes moist. The first of this section to flower for me is this smooth, white form with a greenish tip to the petals. It was grown from seed originally acquired as *N. albidus* var. *kesticus*, a name that has since been amended to *N. cantabricus* subsp. *cantabricus* var. *kesticus*, although in my experience the plant I grow doesn't exhibit the brilliant white colouring you would expect of *N. cantabricus*.

Narcissus 'Chinese Ivory' and 'Silver Palace'

'Chinese Ivory' and 'Silver Palace' are selections from species made by Walter Blom in Oregon USA. Both flower in the middle of winter and I have often taken a pot into the house at Christmas time. 'Chinese Ivory' is a good stable, pale lemon-coloured selection from *N. romieuxii* while 'Silver Palace' is a selection from *N. cantabricus* subsp. *cantabricus* var. *foliosus*.

Growing one clone of a plant in a pot enables a more uniform display of flowers than the wide variations of form and colour often seen in a pot of bulbs grown from seed. Another selection I have made from a pot of *N. romieuxii* seedlings (pictured) is a chalky

N. romieuxii seedling (*all photos* **John Gibson**)

N. romieuxii subsp. *romieuxii* var. *riffanus*

white colour with bags of substance and very smooth, with an even scallop to the corona in the fashion of *N. romieuxii* 'Joy Bishop'.

Narcissus 'Mondieu'

'Mondieu' is a *N. romieuxii* hybrid bred by Rod Barwick of Glenbrook Bulb Farm, Tasmania. It is part of his Little Detective Series, named after Inspector Clouseau's frequent quote 'Mon Dieu'. The large, upward-facing cup is a greatly expanded disc of citrus-yellow; the form is almost petunoid. It has measured up to 55mm (2in) wide, so not a miniature! If the stems are allowed to etiolate, they may need discreet staking to support such a large flower.

Narcissus hedraeanthus

N. hedraeanthus is a distinctive little flower, discovered more than a hundred years ago at Era de Fustal in the province of Jaen. Each bulb carries a solitary leaf that appears alongside the flowers. An unusual feature is the development of the flower stems, which at first lie horizontally, only just above the ground. Eventually the scape straightens out and curves so that the flowers are sometimes carried pointing slightly upwards. The perianth segments, which usually equal the corona in length, are slightly broader with more substance than most bulbocodium, and the colour is a rather pale sulphur-yellow.

N. romieuxii subsp. *romieuxii* var. *riffanus*

N. romieuxii subsp. *romieuxii* var. *riffanus* (pictured) is another fascinating, if somewhat understated, plant. It hails from the Rif mountains in Morocco and the flowers are a smaller version of *N. romieuxii*, with the exception of the poise; on strong erect stems the flowers face upwards to the sky.

Narcissus cantabricus subsp. *cantabricus* var. *petunioides*

Although it's rather a mouthful to say and even more of a pain to write on a plant label, *N. cantabricus* subsp. *cantabricus* var. *petunioides* is the best of the hoop-petticoats in my opinion. The beautiful flowers have a wide, spreading, flat, crystalline white corona that curves away outwards at the margin.

However, the petunoid form does not appear to be stable and seedlings are often variable with not all of them maintaining the desired form.

Therefore, particularly good forms should be selected and grown on as separate clones by crossing these selected forms together. In this way, I have found a higher proportion of the resulting seedlings then maintain the petunoid form. I've made several selections from this species, one with a comparatively large corona that I have tentatively named (but not yet registered) 'Silver Satellite'.

Cultivating winter daffodils

The cultivation cycle for winter daffodils starts in early summer. After the foliage has completely died back, I empty out the pots of bulbs, then clean and inspect individual bulbs before repotting into fresh compost. I use a John Innes No2 soil-based compost[1], to which I add extra grit to assist in the drainage.

I plant them in a mixture of traditional terracotta and modern plastic pots, in a range of sizes from a 80mm (3in) square plastic pot for small single bulbs, up to large Victorian clay pots with three drainage holes for larger *N. papyraceus* and *N. broussonettii* bulbs. The great disparity in the watering requirements of various plants becomes most apparent at the end of the growing season, when a speedy drying out process is required for those bulbs that need a completely dry, warm summer – here terracotta pots are far superior to plastic.

Once re-potted, the pots are kept under cover and dry until the end of summer. Those that require a baking through the summer are set on shelves high up in the greenhouse.

With the approach of autumn and the cooler nights of September, I place all the pots outside on gravel pathways to benefit from the natural autumn rains, to moisten the compost and facilitate root growth. Then, depending on the weather conditions, pots are moved into the greenhouse over a period of weeks. I leave it as late as possible before housing them to allow the foliage to benefit from the natural light and not grow too tall, while I clear out the greenhouse, remove summer shading and clean the greenhouse glass. As light levels rapidly reduce in the long winter nights, maximising the available amount of light to the plants is a priority.

Now that in my area of the East Midlands, snow is less frequent, I've found a way to help simulate the affect of a clear winter's evening after snowfall, when the reflected light from the moon is magnified greatly. I surround my plants with 6mm (¼in) diameter polystyrene beads (as used in bean bags). Spherical in shape, they run fluidly and easily fill voids around pots; providing both insulation against severe cold and raising the ambient light levels.

The British weather is notoriously fickle; on a sunny day even in winter, temperatures can rise rapidly. To mitigate the fluctuation in day/night temperatures, I try to ventilate the greenhouse daily by opening the side louvre windows in all but the most severe weather. Pots of flowering bulbs in the greenhouse need regularly watering and feeding. I make sure the water has stood and acclimatised to the greenhouse temperature before use.

John Gibson *is a well-known daffodil exhibitor, hybridiser and judge; he lectures widely to horticultural societies and is a Vice-Chairman of the RHS Bulb Committee*

NOTES

[1] In the 1930s, research at the John Innes Institute, Surrey, England, led to the creation of a small range of compost that between them were suitable for growing most seeds and plants. Now made by a range of suppliers, the most common John Innes composts are graded 1-3 and consist of seven, three and two parts respectively of loam, peat and sand. Different grades contain successively larger amounts of fertiliser and are designed to provide nutrients for six weeks (Editor).

Surrounding the pots with polystyrene beads helps raise the ambient light levels

Worldwide survey of daffodil breeders

Brian S Duncan

In the 1840s, William Herbert, Dean of Manchester, crossed "a trumpet with a poet" to determine which daffodils should be classed as natural species. The results, which produced flowers with characteristics of both parents, proved that many of those then considered to be species were, in fact, hybrids. As a result a revolution in the development of the daffodil was set in motion.

Herbert was followed by Leeds, Backhouse, Barr and Engleheart. Progress and improvements were so rapid that a mere 60 years after Herbert's experiment the Rev W Wilks (Secretary of the RHS) said: "I doubt if much further advance is now either possible or wanted".

Despite the negative outlook of Rev. W Wilkes, a constant stream of far-seeing breeders have continued to work their magic throughout the 20th century and continue up to the present day.

Major figures of the 20th century including G L Wilson and J L Richardson in Ireland, the Williams cousins, Alec Gray and John Lea in England and Grant E Mitsch in America are no longer with us and in the past ten years at least eleven important daffodil breeders have passed away – Max Hamilton New Zealand 2010; Ian Dyson Australia 2014; Bill Pannill USA 2014; Richard Havens USA 2014; Clive Postles United Kingdom 2016; Kate Reade Northern Ireland 2016; Noel Burr United Kingdom 2017; Walter Blom USA 2018; Fred Silcock Australia 2019; Peter Ramsay New Zealand 2019 and John Pearson United Kingdom 2019.

However, when daffodil enthusiasts get together after the passing of yet another noted breeder, the discussion often turns to thoughts of the future. In considering the age profile of breeders currently active, they start to wonder where the replacements are for those who have passed, who will take on the further development of the genus. Unlike Wilkes, they know that "future advance is both possible and wanted". Improvements in disease resistance and sun-proofing of flowers with coloured coronas are sought. Ambitions also include the injection of red, pink and green into perianths of daffodils. This work is still in its infancy.

Work is already under way to produce miniatures that mirror today's amazing range of colours in standard sized daffodils – a slow process that first involves the creation of many more miniature hybrids that are fertile. This is likely to take several generations to achieve really acceptable results.

It is with such considerations and concerns in mind that the Editorial Committee of this Yearbook thought it would be timely to review the current state of daffodil breeding on a worldwide basis. With this in mind, the following articles have been commissioned from international experts with long experience and personal knowledge of daffodil breeding in their homelands.

Brian S Duncan MBE *is a raiser of a wide range of both standard and miniature daffodils and an enthusiastic student of species daffodils in their natural habitat. Honorary member of the RHS Bulb Committee and past Chairman of the Daffodil and Tulip Committee.*

Australia

Richard Perrignon

Any review of daffodil breeding in Australia since 1970 must begin with the two post-war giants of Tasmanian daffodil breeding, David Jackson and Rod Barwick.

Until their recent retirement, **David and Robin Jackson** were proprietors of Jackson's Daffodils, situated on 16 hectares (40 acres) at Surges Bay, Tasmania, south of Hobart. From about 1970 to 2015, David concentrated on breeding daffodils in divisions 1–4 and 11, always relying on Robin for her sage advice on his selections. He inherited his love of daffodils from his father Tim, who laid the groundwork of the family's breeding programme with some of the best-known Australian exhibition cultivars in divisions 1–4 and himself bred some 368 registered cultivars from 1943 to at least the 1970s, though David continued to register selections up to 1998.

Between about 1985 and 2015, David registered some 432 cultivars, making him the most prolific Australian breeder of exhibition daffodils in the post-war period[1]. His cultivars dominated the Hobart Show annually and other shows throughout Australia and overseas. During his ascendancy, no serious exhibitor could afford to be without them. David was awarded the American Daffodil Society Gold Medal in 1994 and the Peter Barr Memorial Cup by the RHS in 1996. David's hybridising achievements are detailed in my article about him in the 2014 Yearbook. His most famous flowers are the yellow trumpets 'Disquiet' and 'Misquote', bicolor trumpet 'Compute', 'Impeccable' 2Y-Y ,'Terminator' 2Y-R and 'Zombie' 11aW-Y. There's never been another Australian breeder like him.

Rod Barwick is proprietor of Glenbrook Bulb Farm at Claremont in Hobart, Tasmania. There he grows daffodils around his ancestral wood cottage, enjoying an idyllic pasture and orchard covering about 10 hectares (25 acres). As a breeder, Rod has dabbled with standard-sized daffodils with considerable success, but his international reputation has been forged by his miniature creations. Since the 1980s, he has registered 165 cultivars.

He rose to prominence by breeding early blooming hoop petticoat daffodils in the 1980s. By crossing N. bulbocodium subsp. bulbocodium var. conspicuus with N. cantabricus subsp. cantabricus var. foliosus Rod obtained a race of white and primrose hoop petticoats, which have become staples of the show bench in Australia. Among the best of his hoop petticoats to date is 'Mondieu' 10Y-Y, a soft lemon petunioid cultivar bred from N. romieuxii, resembling the Archibolds' selection, 'Julia Jane'.

Rod also followed the example of Alec Gray and Dr Thompson, who bred 'April Tears' 5Y-Y and 'Hawera' 5Y-Y respectively by crossing N. jonquilla with different forms of N. triandrus. Rod used the miniature N. fernandesii rather than N. jonquilla, to produce his 'Angels' series of all-yellow triandrus hybrids. These have dominated the show bench in division 5 in Australia ever since and have gained significant worldwide popularity.

Narcissus 'Voodoo' bred by **Dr Mike Temple-Smith of Launceston** (*all photos* **Richard Perrignon**)

Some of Rod's most distinctive work has been in division 6, producing small hybrids with real character. Outstanding examples have included 'Glenbrook Belle' 6Y-Y and 'The Dansant' 6Y-Y. Among standard-sized daffodils the recently-released 'Elevenses' 11bW-OOY (not registered) and the stunning 'Braes o' Hame' 3W-R (not registered) command attention.

Other notable Tasmanian breeders

• **J M Radcliff** (40 registrations 1940 to 1990) from Tasmania's north. He specialised in divisions 1–3, and is best known for his pink trumpets 'Hawley Rose', 'Rheban Charm' and 'Rubicon Blush' (all 1W-P), and the celebrated stalwarts, 'Rheban Red' 2Y-O and 'Lutana', the almost trumpet 2W-O and key parent of novel 1W-O flowers.

• Retired headmaster and founder of the Tasmanian Daffodil Council, **Harold Cross** DFC (58 registrations 1968 to 1997) bred beautiful doubles including 'Tasrose' 4W-P and 'Tasvention' 4W-O, split-corona daffodils like 'Twotees' 11bW-P/W and elegantly poised daffodils such as 'Possum' 3W-P.

• **Dr Mike Temple-Smith** of Launceston (48 registrations 1990 to 2015) worked mainly with standard-sized daffodils and produced some very pretty flowers, like 'Tannatea' 2W-WWP and 'Poykokarra' 3W-YYO. He is chiefly remembered for crossing 'Ristin' 1Y-Y with *N. cyclamineus* to produce a refined trio of intermediate-sized division 6 cultivars, including the celebrated 'Abracadabra' and 'Voodoo' (pictured), both 6Y-Y.

• Mike's father, **Geoff Temple-Smith** (ten registrations 1980s to 2003) is chiefly remembered for his miniature 'Nodding Acquaintance' 7Y-Y and his Waterfall series: 'Liffey Falls', 'Snug Falls' and 'Russell Falls', (pictured) all registered 5Y-Y.

• J M Radcliff's son **Peter (Jamie) Radcliff** (eleven registrations 1990 to the present) has registered daffodils in divisions 1, 2 and 11 and is best known for orange trumpet 'Tarkine' 1W-OOY (named after the

N. 'Russell Falls' is part of Geoff Temple-Smith's Waterfalls series

Tasmanian wilderness) and sizzling large-cup 'Hawley Gift' 2Y-R.

• **Kevin Crowe** (16 registrations 1995 to the present) works with miniatures. Inspired by Rod Barwick. Kevin lives with his wife Mary at Austin's Ferry, Hobart, and breeds his daffodils in an area not much exceeding 6m^2 (7.2yd^2). His ultra-miniature hybrids 'Cazwhite' and 'Cazblonde' (both 6W-W), and 'Frisson', 'Mehmet' and 'Min' (all 6 Y-Y) are achieving show successes and renown.

• **Don Broadfield** (17 registrations 1985 to 2007) including 'Lady Diana' 2W-W (not registered).

• **Owen Davies** (15 registrations 2015 to 2018) is founder and organiser of the All Saints show at Hobart, the latest daffodil show in the country.

Mainland Australia – prominent Victorian breeders since the 1980s

• **Hancock's Daffodils** at Menzies Creek in the Dandenong Mountains outside Melbourne (774 registrations, 1945 [2] to date) is the oldest and largest specialty daffodil supplier in Australia. It was founded during the First World War by English expatriate Harold Brown and has passed through several hands. It is now owned by Will Ashburner, formerly of Digger's Seeds, and his wife Christine.

The firm supplies decorative and garden cultivars of their own breeding, and the work of other Australian and overseas breeders.

• **Lindsay Dettman** of Kyneton (143 registrations 1978 to 1989) was a friend of the Murray and Miller farming families and a stalwart of the Kyneton Show. Delicately rimmed 'Janelle' 3W-YYR was his last registration and one of his prettiest.

• **Evelyn Murray** (25 registrations 1940 to 2000) from Kyneton in the central highlands of Victoria produced very pretty flowers in divisions 1-3, at her 400 hectare (1,000 acre) farm Langley Vale. She had a particular interest in pink daffodils and is famous for 'My Word'. Despite suffering from Parkinson's disease Eve was always a warm and generous hostess, and I remember her fondly.

• **Ian Dyson** (21 registrations 2005 to 2015) was proprietor of Classic Daffodils at Leongatha, south west of Melbourne. His greatest successes included the splendid pink trumpet 'My Fair Lady' (not registered) and yellow-pink confection 'Coral Isle'. On Ian's death, most of his seedlings were transferred to Hancock's, where they are being evaluated.

• **Fred Silcock** of Mount Macedon (eight registrations 1990 to 2015) produced tens of thousands seedlings in divisions 1–4 and 6, including 'Timberman' 2W-Y and 'Perchance' 6W-YPP. Fred gardened on about two hectares (five acres) at Mount Macedon, but planted his seedlings on nearby farms with permission from farmers. Though among the most prolific Australian breeders ever, he registered few cultivars, gave away many and sold none. His obituary is in the 2019 Yearbook (pp72–3).

• **Graeme Brumley** (ten registrations to date from the 1990s to the present) breeds daffodils at Kyneton in Victoria, specialising in divisions 1–3. His work includes the stunning pink large-cup 'Warrambine' and 'Narracan', a wonderfully smooth gold trumpet.

• **Michael Spry** (195 registrations 1949 to the 1970s, though people kept registering his work until 1998).

• **C O Fairbairn** (40 registrations 1940 to 1980) from the Western Districts of Victoria is best remembered for 'Mrs David Calvert' 3WGRR (not registered).

• **Oscar Ronalds** (65 registrations 1920 to the 1970s, though people kept registering his work until 2010), is best known for 'Golden Robin' 1Y-Y and 'Welcome Inn' 2Y-Y, which I believe is sold in Australia as 'Welcome' (unregistered).

• **Rev E W Philpot** (27 registrations from 1959 to the 1970s, though people kept registering his seedlings until 2008) is best known for 'Polar Imp' 3W-W.

Mainland Australia – prominent 21st-century New South Wales raisers

In the past 25 years, a significant trio of breeders in Canberra has emerged.

• Retired school teacher **Lawrence Trevanion** (50 registrations 2000 to date) grows daffodils in suburban Canberra, and on about 16 hectares (40 acres) at Marchmont, near Yass. Following Glenbrook's example, Lawrence has become perhaps Australia's most prolific breeder of hoop petticoat daffodils. Outstanding among them is his large, early primrose petunioid 'Quen Dor'. He is also famous for his split-corona standard-sized 'Triple Tiger' 11Y-Y, which is his multi-headed answer to 'Tripartite' and 'Splatter'. Possibly his greatest achievements – though unrecognised on the show bench because of their earliness – are his division 8 hybrids, particularly his ground-breaking hybrid of *N. elegans*, 'First Stanza' 8W-O, and allotetraploid 'Nomatta' 8Y-Y (not registered). His work is profiled in the 2019 Yearbook (pp16–21).

• Father and son team **Tony and Graeme Davis** (30 registrations between them, 1995 to date), of Burradoo and Canberra respectively, specialise in divisions 1–3, 8, 9 and 11, producing some real beauties such as 'Jumbuck' 1Y-O and 'Bundanoon' 2W-P. More recent 'Miss Rhiannon' with its extraordinary biscuit-coloured rim regularly takes championships at the Canberra Show.

• Recently retired government lawyer **Graeme**

Lawrence Trevanion from Canberra has already made 50 registrations since 2000

Fleming of Keira Bulbs (11 registrations 1995 to date) breeds daffodils on two hectares (five acres) in the nursery precinct on the outskirts of Canberra. Though he also breeds standard-sized daffodils, Graeme produces exquisite miniatures that have earned the 'most awarded' prize at the Canberra Show year after year and an enviable international reputation. Outstanding among his creations are 'Papa Snoz' 6Y-Y and 'Second Fiddle' 6W-Y. In my view, the best of Graeme's work is still under number and awaiting registration.

What of the future?

Of the 25 breeders described (counting Hancock's as one), only 11 are still with us, and only 4 – Hancock's, Glenbrook Bulb Farm, Trevanion Daffodils and Keira Bulbs – sell their work on anything like a commercial scale. Of those four, three are best known for their work with miniatures, and though at least two breed exhibition cultivars in

divisions 1–4, neither specialises in them.

Consequently, for the foreseeable future, Australian output will probably continue to cover the gamut of decorative and exhibition cultivars, but the higher divisions and miniatures are likely to dominate the latter.

Of the 11 still with us, most are considerably older than me and I turned 60 last year. The future of daffodils here, of course, belongs to them. Regrettably, in the past 15 years there has been a dearth of younger breeders with anything like the vigour of the older growers, at least on the mainland. The situation is better in Tasmania, where up- and-coming growers like the Nobles and Owen Davies offer hope for the future, and new exhibitors continue to appear. Even so, sadly, the wind that blew so strongly after the War, and billowed the sails of the exhibition daffodil movement in Australia, has calmed.

Those who are inoculated with 'gold fever' rarely if ever recover from the disease, so the movement probably has another decade or two left in it, unless the culture of 'instant gratification' engendered by social media and modern living is replaced by something less ephemeral. A lot can change, of course, in 20 years. Time will tell.

Richard Perrignon *has covered the Australian daffodil season for the RHS for more than 25 years. He studied plant science at university, has published research in Acta Horticulturae, has worked as a horticultural journalist and photographer and is a barrister*

NOTES

[1] Numbers of registrations reflect the entries on Daffseek.org for any particular breeder. As Daffseek also lists daffodils not registered with the RHS, in some cases the number of RHS registrations may be fewer.
[2] Brown sold his daffodil business to Hancock in 1945. From 1933 to 1965, 244 daffodils were registered in Brown's name, separately from Hancock's.

England

Reg Nicholl

Daffodil breeding commenced in the early 19th century in mainland Britain when the likes of polymath Dean William Herbert (1778–1847) whose work in deliberate cross-pollination to produce new hybrids laid the spadework for two men. **Edward Leeds** (1802–1877), a stockbroker from Manchester, who began his pollinating in 1843, and **William Backhouse** (1807–1869), a banker from Wolsingham, Durham, following on some 20 years later, are widely regarded as the developers of the modern daffodil.

In their wake at the turn of the 20th century came one of the most prolific breeders of all time, **Rev George Engleheart** (1851–1936), who registered well over 700 cultivars. In 1912 the Royal Horticultural Society honoured his handiwork by presenting for competition, the Engleheart Cup for twelve cultivars bred and raised by the exhibitor.

Cornwall was also in the forefront of breeding, and miniature daffodil specialist **Alec Gray** (1895–1986) is famed for his 'Tête-à- tête', which is potted up in millions

John W Blanchard's 'Crevette'
(*all photos* **Michael Baxter**)

each year by the Dutch bulb industry.

The **Williams** cousins, **John Charles** (1861–1939) and **Percival Dacres** (1865–1935) were also prolific, with the latter registering hundreds of his own flowers. **Robert Backhouse** (1854–1940) and his wife **Sarah** (1857–1921) raised more than 600 cultivars between them and were responsible for perhaps the first 'pink' daffodil named 'Mrs. R. O. Backhouse' 2W-P.

Modern-day breeders

- **Mrs J (Barbara) Abel Smith** (1914–1995) registered 107 daffodils. Based in Letty Green, Hertfordshire, her bloom of 'Park Springs' 3W-WWY is probably her best known, but a couple of all-white flowers – 'April Love' 1W-W with immaculate form but 'difficult' to maintain and 'Tutankhamun' 2W- GWW – have had many show bench successes.
- **John W Blanchard** VMH (1930–) registered 52 cultivars, many of them miniatures. His introduction of 'Crevette' 8W-O ('Mahmoud' × *N. dubius*) (pictured) was the first miniature to feature a colour other than yellow or white in the corona and was the initial winner of the Ralph B White Memorial Medal for innovative daffodils. His other superb miniatures include 'Pequenita' 7Y-Y, 'Miss Klein' 7Y-Y and 'Peseta' 8W-Y while 'Badbury Rings' 3Y-YYR and 'Purbeck' 3W-YOO are outstanding among his excellent standard-sized cultivars. He was the first exhibitor to stage twelve miniature cultivars in the Engleheart Cup.
- **F E (Freddie) Board** (1902–1966) holds the record for the registration of cultivars when, in one year, 1965, he forwarded no less than 125 to the International Daffodil Registrar. Among his cultivars that have stood the test of time are 'Strines' 2Y-Y, 'Altruist' 3O-R and two excellent division 2 all-whites 'Misty Glen' and 'Broomhill'.
- **Noel A Burr** (1930–2017) named 58 cultivars including elegant 'Cherrygardens' 2W-WPP, 'Finchcocks' 2Y-R and 'Saxonbury' 2Y-Y. He received the Ralph B White Medal in 2004 for 'Dunstan's Fire' 1Y-O and claimed to

'Eastbrook Sunrise' raised by John Gibson

'Astrid's Memory' was bred by Clive A Postles

have won the Engleheart Cup from just three 7.3 × 0.9m (24 × 3ft) plots in his back garden.
• **Barbara Fry** BEM (1922–1997) was hardly known outside daffodil circles but she bred 93 cultivars that her employer, the Rosewarne Experimental Horticultural Station in Camborne, Cornwall, registered to replace ageing and declining daffodil stocks. Known to her friends as 'Bob', 'Bob Minor' 1Y-Y and 'Small Fry' 1Y-Y were named after her.
• **John Gibson** (1950–) raises flowers on an allotment rented from no less than the Duke of Buccleuch and has registered 40 cultivars to date. John has produced a number of splendid flowers such as 'Corby Candle' 2Y-YOO, which is proving to be one of the best in its class. 'Eastbrook Sunrise' (pictured) is a fine addition to the rather scarce 1Y-O section and 'Grafton Gold' 2Y-Y to the burgeoning group of intermediate-sized daffodils.
• **E G B (Eddie) Jarman** (1933–) is another amateur winner of the Ralph B White Medal (1999) with his bright red-rimmed 'Garden Party' 2W-WRR. His registrations include the superb 'Happy Valley' 2Y-Y, 'Warm Welcome' 2W-GWP and all-orange 'Ruddy Duck' 2O-O.
• **John S B Lea** (1911–1984) registered 135 cultivars all of excellent quality and is undoubtedly the doyen of English hybridists in this period. It is almost impossible to select a few of his flowers as he set new standards for form, size and brilliance of colour with his

uncanny skill in choosing parents for his cross-pollinating. His 'Canisp' 2W-W, 'Achduart' 3Y-O, 'Dailmanach' 2W-P, 'Gold Convention' 2Y-Y and 'Glenfarclas' 1Y-O are a fair representation together with the 24 flowers named after Scottish lochs that were his forte. He won the Engleheart Cup on no fewer than eleven occasions.
• **A J R (John) Pearson** (1936–2019) bred 101 daffodils including the outstanding 'Altun Ha' 2YYW-W, which, along with 'Sargeant's Caye' 1YYW-WWY and 'Lighthouse Reef' 1YYW-WWY, revolutionised divisions 1 and 2 reverse-bicolor cultivars. Distinctive 'Clouded Yellow' 2YYW-Y was his personal favourite and 'Sheelagh Rowan' 2W-W is proving to be really special, particularly in New Zealand.
• **Clive A Postles** (1937–2016) registered 167 cultivars. Mentored by John Lea, Clive has emulated the master and produced three of the leading flowers in their respective classes in 'Ombersley' 1Y-Y, 'Crowndale' 4Y-O and, one of the finest flowers to date, 'Astrid's Memory' 3W-Y (pictured). He also produced excellent cultivars in a section badly needing new blood, division 1 bicolors 'Bramcote Gem' and 'Bramcote Daybreak'. One in the same division named after him may well prove to be the best. A tribute to his daffodil legacy is included in the 2019 Yearbook, pp34–37.
• **Ronald A Scamp** (1943–) is the most prolific modern breeder with 372 cultivars

registered. He is largely responsible for the wider acceptance of split-corona daffodils with his first class 'Boslowick' 11aY-O, 'Menehay' 11a-Y-O and 'Jack Wood' 11aY-Y (pictured). 'Blisland' 9W-YYR and 'Cape Cornwall' 2Y-YYO are among the leaders in their classes.

• Other breeders who have raised significant cultivars include: Michael Baxter, 'Lakeland Fair' 2W-GPP (pictured); Frank Verge, 'Fiona MacKillop' 2W-Y; Tony Noton, 'Citronita' a breakthrough all-yellow division 3; J M 'Toty' de Navarro, 'Estremadura' 2Y-O; Michael Jefferson-Brown, 'Hero' 1Y-O; Dennis Milne, 'Sabine Hay' 3O-R; June Pesterfield, 'Dandubar' 7Y-Y (Ralph White Medal 2003); David Lloyd, 'Beauvallon' 4Y-ORR; Arthur Robinson, 'Bailey' 2O-0; George Tarry, 'Jamage' – perhaps the most northerly raised tazzeta hybrid; Jan Dalton, 'Miller Howe' 6Y-Y; Malcolm Bradbury, 'Majestic Gold' 1Y-Y; Alec Harper, 'Churchfield Bells' 5Y-Y (pictured); Paul Payne, 'Ranworth Broad' 2Y-R; Rae Beckwith, 'Will's Yellow' 3Y-Y; Anne Wright, 'Giselle' 10W-W; Chris Yates, 'Kantzeewai' 2Y-YPP; and Richard Brook, multi-headed all-yellow split-corona 'Tripartite' 11aY-Y, his only registration, is now being grown in the Netherlands.

Scotland and Wales

The only major modern breeder in Scotland was **Dugald C MacArthur** (1927–2018), who registered 187 cultivars for the commercial market. Otherwise, hybridising appears to be confined to alpine bulb enthusiasts Ian Young in Scotland and Rannveig Wallis in Wales.

The future

The prospect for British daffodil breeding looks distinctly bleak as most of the few excellent breeders that remain have already reached three score and ten. There is Jeremy Wilkes in his fifties, who has made a great start with his successful intermediate- sized 'Winks' 2Y-YOO ('Badbury Rings' × 'Bailey') (pictured) but I don't know of any others.

'Jack Wood'

'Lakeland Fair'

'Churchfield Bells'

'Winks'

Germany

N. x xanthochlorus (N. cavanillesii x N. viridiflorus)
(*all photos* **Theo Sanders**)

Theo Sanders

Germany has no tradition of exhibiting daffodils and the only daffodil hybridisers we have are Petra Vogt and myself.

Petra Vogt

Petra Vogt, born 1963, has grown many types of daffodils in a small backyard garden for about 20 years. She makes about 10 to 20 crosses each year, with about 20 to 80 seeds from each cross. Her breeding focus is on the small-cupped pink daffodils, which, despite their special charm and beauty, in her view have been neglected by most breeders in the past. Emphasis is on snow-white perianths and short cups of clear true pink without much yellowish undertones. As many division 3 daffodils are late flowering due to their close relation to *N. poeticus*, early flowering of her seedlings is another desired feature.

A few of her second and third generation seedlings, bred from 3 W-W cultivars crossed with rather short-cupped division 2 pink ('Elizabeth Ann' × 'Fairy Magic') × ('Irish Linen' × 'Clouds Rest') (pictured), are close to her targets and suitable for exhibition. Many selections are smallish or intermediate – good garden plants that fit well in a natural environment. Petra is confident that soon her seedling beds will offer up some nice surprises.

Theo Sanders

I worked as a professor of Material Science at the University of Duisburg/Essen and began breeding daffodils in 1973 on a small scale. I now have a field of 1500m² (1,793yd² square yards) with frost-resistant daffodils and 20m² (24yd²) with 520 pots of species and hybrids under glass. I make about 150 to 250 crosses per year and about half set seed. The main breeding goals are:

- Little white, yellow or coloured daffodils with more than one flower per stem. Flowers can also be double or have split-coronas.
- Chromosome doubling of species and species hybrids.
- Jonquilla and Viridiflorus hybrids and their crosses with species.
- Allotetraploid varieties of crosses from standard daffodils with *N. bulbocodium* and *N. cavanillesii*.
- Frost-resistant Tazetta hybrids and crosses with 'Matador'.
- Rapid-growing Triandrus hybrids.
- Species hybrids eg *N. × xanthochlorus* (pictured).
- Crosses of standard-sized daffodils with species – 'Quasar' × *N. gaditanus*' (pictured)

'Quasar' x *N. gaditanus*

N. ('Elizabeth Ann' x 'Fairy Magic') x ('Irish Linen' x 'Clouds Rest')

I have registered only a few of my daffodils. This year I shall do this for the tetraploid forms of 'Hawera' and 'Fairy Chimes', which I generated by chromosome doubling. The first crosses with these plants have flowered ('Ice Chimes' × 'Fairy Chimes' [tetraploid]') (pictured). Seventeen promising varieties are planted and under trial by Arno Kroon in the Netherlands. He seeks especially daffodils that are suitable for use as pot plants. One aspirant is the cross 'Hillstar' × N. *hedraeanthus*.

For hybridising, both the seed parent and the pollen parent must be fertile. Often the descendants of a cross are infertile but some of the plants have a low fertility, which is sufficient to make further crosses. The question is: Which constitutions have the gametes? I have suggested some solutions to this problem in my articles, which can be found in the American Daffodil Society's 'DaffLibrary' or on www.theo-sanders-daffodils.de. This genetic background is not only important for breeding daffodils but also for hybridising other flowers, vegetables, fruits and cereals.

'Ice Chimes' x 'Fairy Chimes'

Ireland

James Akers

I have been personally involved with daffodils for most of the five decades considered in this review of worldwide breeding activity. However, although now a regular visitor to daffodil shows in Northern Ireland and, despite accompanying my late wife Wendy when she judged in Belfast almost 25 years ago, I never met several of the people mentioned below. The Northern Ireland

Daffodil Group booklet *Daffodils in Ireland* published in 1998 has been used to provide the information which I lacked.

The following table is an analysis (using Daffseek, the American Daffodil Society online daffodil database), of the number of cultivars raised by hybridisers from Ireland and registered during the past 50 years. Any registered cultivars from previous years are also shown – Guy L Wilson and W J (Willy) Dunlop, neighbours and friends from Broughshane, County Antrim were the major breeders just before the period reviewed Hybridisers who registered just one or two cultivars in the early years are excluded, but the data for this century is complete.

Cultivars raised by hybridisers from Ireland and registered during the past 50 years

Breeder	<1970	1971–80	1981–90	1991–00	2001–10	2011–20	Total
Guy L Wilson	654	7	–	–	–	–	661
WJ Dunlop	134	3	–	–	–	–	137
Lionel & Helen Richardson	695	136	23	1	–	1	856
Sir Frank Harrison	22	55	76	55	5	4	217
Carncairn Daffodils	22	68	75	40	4	1	210
Tom Bloomer	96	34	43	–	1	–	174
Brian s Duncan	–	76	180	178	211	206	851
Nial Watson	–	–	–	–	7	53	60
Derrick Turbitt	–	–	–	–	2	5	7
Richard McCaw	–	–	–	–	3	–	3
Maurice Kerr	–	–	–	–	–	3	3
Totals	1,623	379	397	274	233	273	3,179

Republic of Ireland

Six raisers registered daffodils during the past 50 years, none of whom are alive today. Three amateur exhibitors, **Michael J Ward, Dr J G D (Keith) Lamb** and **Patrick Kiernan** registered just seven cultivars between them, while 161 other cultivars were registered by **J Lionel Richardson and/or his wife Helen**. In all 856 cultivars were raised between 1914 and Helen's death in 1978. Lionel was a very keen and successful exhibitor in the whole of Ireland and at RHS and Midland Daffodil Society shows in England until his death in 1961. It is interesting to note that all breeders on the list can trace links all the way back to William Baylor Hartland and Miss Fanny Currey from County Cork at the turn of the 19th century. These two pioneered visits to RHS and Midland Daffodil Society shows in England that continue to this day.

J L and Mrs H K Richardson, Waterford
Analysis of all flowers raised

Division	1	2	3	4	6	9	Total
Registered	170	458	119	100	8	1	856

Northern Ireland

Ballydorn Bulb Farm, Killinchy, Co Down
Sir Frank and Lady Harrison's involvement with daffodils began shortly after the end of the Second World War. The two hectare (five acre) farm was used to produce daffodils for the cut flower trade after advice from Guy L Wilson and Lionel Richardson who also provided the bulbs. The business expanded and large quantities of excess bulbs were sold. Breeding of new cultivars started to provide early-flowering cultivars for the cut flower trade and provide 'novelties' for bulb sales.

The analysis of flowers raised reflects the preference of general garden customers and exhibitors at the time, focusing on cultivars from Divisions 1–3. However, Sir Frank's personal preference was for poeticus cultivars. Of these the best known are 'Fanad Head', 'Frank's Fancy' both 9W-GYR and 'Green Lodge' 9W-GGO. Closely related to the poets were the 3W-GYR pair 'Lisbane' and 'Tullybeg', both grown in quantity in the Netherlands.

Division	1	2	3	4	6	9	Total
Registered	25	83	82	2	4	21	217

Carncairn Daffodils, Broughshane, Co Antrim
Carncairrn Daffodils was a bulb-selling
business set up in 1956 by Kate Reade and her
husband Robin, again with the help and advice
of Guy L Wilson. There was an early
recognition of the need for new cultivars and
the first registration was in 1967. Among
those registered in 1969 was the beautiful
flower 'Foundling', a division 6, but whose
form was not readily accepted by some purists
who termed it an 'Irish Cyclamineus'.

Division	1	2	3	4	6	7	Total
Registered	32	120	39	15	3	1	210

Tom Bloomer, Ballymena, County Antrim
Unlike the two raisers from the North above,
whose purpose was to provide new cultivars
for their business, Tom Bloomer was an
amateur hybridiser. With the need to
landscape the one hectare (two and a half
acres) of land at his new home just before the
Second World War, he turned for advice to a
neighbour, Guy L Wilson. Unsurprisingly
therefore he became a most successful

daffodil exhibitor, including in the middle
1950s winning the Bowles Cup in London
three years in a row.

He made his first cross in 1950 and in the
period until 1973 he made 869 crosses and
sowed 14,954 seeds. Wherever possible in his
showing career he preferred to exhibit flowers
of his own raising. His best known cultivars
were his white trumpets 'Silent Valley' and
'White Star', both of which have many Best
Bloom awards to their credit.

Division	1	2	3	9	Total
Registered	37	80	55	2	174

Brian S Duncan, Omagh, County Tyrone
Although having a long involvement with the
commercial side of daffodil growing,
competitive exhibition has been the dominant
factor in Brian's breeding programme and
aims. His first serious crosses were made in
1964 and the first five registrations were from
four different divisions, a versatility which
continued as I believe he is the only raiser to
have registered cultivars from all twelve of the

**Brian S Duncan has planted almost 300,000 seeds
in his 56 years of hybridising and among his 851
introductions are 'Seville Orange' (left) and
'Silver Pearls (below)** (*photos* **Brian Duncan**)

hybrid divisions. His main ambition when he began was to win the Engleheart Cup, which he has achieved many times over. Coloured trumpets in division 1 and all-pink daffodils are continuing aims.

'Prime Target', 'Garden Beacon' and 'Seville Orange' (pictured) are examples of his 1W-O flowers, the former two having been awarded the RHS Ralph White Memorial Medal for innovation. However, over the past 20 years his breeding programme has favoured miniature daffodils. As a result, in 2018 he won the Engleheart Cup with twelve miniatures from six different divisions, surely his most outstanding success as an exhibitor. His sole division 8 registration is a miniature cultivar, 'Silver Pearls' (pictured), 'Good Try' and 'Winning Try' both 5Y-Os are perhaps his best attempts to inject colour into miniature daffodils. Brian's records of crosses and seed counts show that he has made nearly 4,000 crosses and planted almost 300,000 seeds in the 56 years he has been hybridising.

Division	1	2	3	4	5	6	Total
Registered	121	354	141	83	25	65	
Division	7	8	9	10	11	12	
Registered	15	1	12	5	21	8	851

Nial Watson, Killinchy, County Down

Interest in daffodils began 25 years ago after meeting breeder Sir Frank Harrison. He helped him at Ballydorn Bulb Farm and made his first tentative crosses in the late 1990s.

Strong healthy plants are a top priority from all divisions but Nial has long been keen on miniatures and intermediates. One aim is to have rimmed cultivars in all divisions (see 'Volcanic Fire'), along with all-pink cultivars and colour in miniatures. Intermediate 'Little Alice' 4Y-O, named for his daughter has had great success and in 2014 'Cut Crystal' 11aW-W received the Ralph White Memorial Medal.

Division	1	2	3	4	5	6	9	11	Total
Registered	5	18	16	8	1	1	5	6	60

'Volcanic Fire' (photo Nial Watson)

Derrick Turbitt, Portstewart, County Antrim

Derrick became involved with daffodils in the 1980s under the influence of Dave Willis, developer of the Guy Wilson Memorial Gardens in Coleraine and started hybridising soon after. The main breeding interests are standard daffodils in divisions 1 to 4, 6 and 11, plus miniatures and intermediates.

A keen and successful exhibitor, his original targets were for flowers with smooth petals and bright colours, but now the elusive 1W-O. 'Causeway Sunset' (pictured) is his most successful cultivar – the prefix due to living close to the Giant's Causeway at Bushmills.

Division	1	2	3	6	Total
Registered	1	3	2	1	7

'Causeway Sunset' (photo Ian Scroggy)

Richard McCaw and Maurice Kerr have been active raisers for over 25 years, but growing problems have limited their success. Details can be found in Daffodils in Ireland (pp94 and 99). Richard has made 3 registrations, all division 3; Maurice has made 2 registrations from divisions 3 and 1 from division 4

Conclusion

With the demise of six of the hybridisers on the summary list above and the fact that practically all the remaining active breeders are well into their retirement years it seems that the long tradition of daffodil breeding in Ireland may be coming to an end.

Dave Hardy of Esker Farm Daffodils started hybridising in 2013 and he is now making about 75 crosses per year with preferences for intermediates, miniatures and poeticus varieties. So, it remains for Dave, a Lancastrian married to an Ulster girl, to rescue the situation and it is hoped he can influence other younger people to get involved with daffodils. That is a big ask in these modern times of instant gratification.

James Akers *was a member of the RHS Daffodil and Tulip Committee (now Bulb Committee) for many years and is an exhibitor of English Florists' Tulips and Miniature Daffodils*

Japan

Brian S Duncan

For this symposium I have been unable to find a contributor from Japan. My business records show that we had 25 enthusiastic Japanese customers in 2000 and I know that some of these people expressed interest in daffodil breeding and bought cultivars especially for this purpose. However, I only have contact with Junjiro and Yoshiko Miyata with whom we still exchange season's greetings.

Knowing of the undoubted interest in

daffodils in Japan it was a surprise to find that only 14 daffodil cultivar names are listed in Daffseek, all bred by the aforementioned **Junjiro Miyata** between 2002 and 2017. They cover four divisions and his 'Asahi' 2Y-YYO is in tribute to the brand/brewery of which he was CEO.

Daffodil names in Japanese script can be found on the Internet and the RHS has a National Registrar (Japan) but it seems that Japanese breeders are not registering their daffodil names in English. This is understandable, if their daffodil creations are confined to their home market but as International Daffodil Registration Authority we should continue to encourage appropriate registration in all countries.

New Zealand

Graham J Phillips
and Denise McQuarrie

Daffodil hybridising has been going on in New Zealand for over 100 years with more than 60 enthusiasts registering 4,745 cultivars including 2,200 in the past 50 years. Vast improvements have been made in that time.

Currently 27 people are hybridising at a modest level and a dozen more with a more extreme expression of 'hybriditis'. We record some details of the activities and successes of the 50 percent who responded to us. Our most venerable respondent, John Hunter, has been hybridising for 70+ years with others raising for about 20 years or much longer.

The number of crosses made obviously varies from year to year. Some hybridists make 10 or 20 crosses per year and those with severe 'hybriditis' create 100+ crosses, resulting in anything from about 100+ seeds per cross to just a few seeds; all amounting to thousands of seeds per year. The survey indicates that annually more than 600 crosses are currently being made in New Zealand. Our respondents report success rates from as little as 30 to nearly 100 percent, occurring before these seedlings produce their first flower. Losses occur due to poor germination, pest and disease or even neglect, but enough survive to ensure a continuing parade of improved and innovative cultivars. Attention is focused on divisions 1–4 but specialists are also doing great work with intermediates, miniatures, tazettas, poets, split-corona daffodils and the other higher divisions. Special attention is being given to intensifying corona colour in trumpet daffodils and the red/pinks in all divisions. Great progress has been made with double daffodils by improving stem strength and consistency.

This is an attempt to record the activities of some of our current crop of hybridisers whose efforts are making improvements to those exhibition cultivars already available.

North Island
Robin Hill, Waikato
Trading as Fisher Nurseries, Robin took over Ramsay Daffodils' collection five years ago. His own breeding programme has recently concentrated on yellow/pink and bicolor trumpet crosses with several excellent 2Y-R and 2Y-Y seedlings. Robin has bred quite a few miniatures and still makes crosses in this field. He aims to make 40–50 crosses each season.

Graham Phillips, Hamilton
Growing and hybridising daffodils since the early 1970s, Graham has made thousands of crosses and registered 63 cultivars. Recent interest has been in raising improved pink/red seedlings in divisions 1–4 and some of his best are 'Luvit' 2W-R (pictured), 'Ruby Duby' 2W-R and 'Pink Quest' 3W-WWP (pictured).

His special interest are 3W-Ps and Graham reckons he has some 'yummy' things among 30 or more such selections under trial. As a commercial cut flower grower Graham has also bred a lot of super-early yellow and yellow/red flowers after five or six generations

'Luvit' is among Graham Phillips' 63 registered cultivars (*all photos* **Graham Phillips**)

'Pink Quest' introduced by Graham Phillips

of persistent crossing, thus extending the season from 10 to almost 20 weeks. Doubles are another focus, seeking strong stems, short necks and good form. His seedling U97-1 is a 4W-P that's receiving much attention. Graham still makes 100 crosses per year, so there's a lot yet to come from the Phillips fields.

Graeme and Faith Miller, Waikato

Graeme and Faith Miller trade as Miller Daffodils. Graeme dabbled with hybridising as a teenager and really got into it in 1984, along with Faith. They have attempted to hybridise across all divisions and registered 101 cultivars – an eclectic collection including standard, Intermediate and miniature-sized daffodils. Notable flowers include 'Coconut Cream' 2W-W, cool lemon-coloured 'Lemon Smoothie' 2Y-Y and unusual 'Frontier Glow' 2Y-O, which attains an apricot glow as it matures. They have reduced to about 40 crosses per year. Graeme believes that seeing the flower of a good new seedling for the first time is the ultimate daffodil patch experience.

Wayne Hughes, Whanganui

Wayne Hughes, on the west coast, specialises in intermediates, a section that has been gaining popularity in recent years. He has also registered some fine standard-sized daffodils including 'Crystal Gem' 2W-W and 'Sandmere Gold' 2Y-Y, both among the very best in their respective divisions. Wayne has registered 16 intermediates and 'Tayforth Small One' 2Y-O, 'Tayforth Joy' 2Y-YOO and 'Tayforth May' 2Y-O are some of his finest.

Spud Brogden, Taranaki

Spud Brogden started hybridising with his Dad (GWE Brogden) in 1954, but only seriously with recorded crosses in 1978. In good years he would make up to 120 crosses that resulted in up to 2,000 seeds. The crosses were mainly for exhibition flowers in divisions 1–3 and his wonderful cultivars include standout 'Kiwi Happy Prince' 2W-YYO. Spud is now well into his eighties, and red/orange perianths are a prime interest. He has his unflowered seedlings and a small collection and still exhibits at National shows.

John McLennan, Otaki

John McLennan is a commercial cut-flower grower whose influence is seen in the beautiful doubles on which he has concentrated with such success. His 'Ballistic' 4Y-R, first seen at the South Island Show in 2009, has been hard to beat. It is widely grown now as it is such a fast multiplier. Also notable are 'Lucky Dice' 4Y-Y, a lovely full symmetrical late bloomer; 'Neavesville Gold', a very neat 4Y-Y; 'Otaki Legacy' 4Y-O; and the little well-named Intermediate 'Brass Button' 4Y-Y, often on the Premier table. John has bred daffodils in other divisions including division 8. I especially like 'Smitten' 2W-P, which is a delicious colour and a valuable addition to the pinks.

Wilfred Hall, Kapiti Coast

Wilfred Hall has concentrated on tazettas, poets and jonquil hybrids and has bred most division 8 blooms on the show bench today. Of his registered 25 tazettas, 'Avalex' 8W-Y is perhaps the most widely grown and successful. 'Harpswell' 8W-Y, 'Abraxis' 8W-O and 'Lemon and Barley' 8Y-Y are excellent, as is 'Fencourt Jewel', that marvellous 8W-P.

Jonquils such as 'Delltone' 7Y-O, 'Elfina'

Max Hamilton's 'Thumbs Up' (above left)
and Peter Ramsay's 'Cameo Joy' (above right)
(*photos* **Michael Baxter**)

7W-P and 'Yellow Dello' 7Y-YOO have made their mark, while regular winner 'Eskedos' 2Y-R is a wonderful little intermediate – brightly coloured, smooth and immaculate.

Max Hamilton and Peter Ramsay, Koanga Daffodils

These two prolific hybridisers of recent years are unfortunately no longer with us. The obituaries for Max Hamilton and Peter Ramsay of Koanga Daffodils can be found in the 2011 and 2019 Yearbooks, respectively. Max's best known are 'Rongoiti Gem' 4W-O and 'Thumbs Up' 2Y-O (pictured) in addition to his many poets. Among Peter's best are white double 'Ameeya' and 'Cameo Joy' 2Y-R (pictured) – both with Best Bloom awards.

South Island
John Hunter, Nelson

Now is in his mid-eighties, John, with the help of his wife Marie, continues on with his collection and is still doing about 30 crosses every year. John made his first cross is 1949 and has done every year since, last year being his 70th year of hybridising. John has hybridised in every division and has registered 160 marvellous cultivars. 'Cosmic Ice' 1W-W, 'Luminosity' 2YYW-Y, which is hard to beat in its class, 'Pink Cosmos' 1W-P and

'Hunterston' 3W-GYR are some of the best recent registrations. A 6Y-W bred from his 'Flight Path' excites him as he believes it is the best cyclamineus he has ever seen. John also has some excellent doubles and ground-breaking viridiflorus hybrids. Like Spud he is now concentrating on red perianth crosses. John is a true statesman of daffodils.

Mike Smith, Motueka

Mike Smith has been breeding predominantly split-corona daffodils since 2003. He sows about 250 seeds per year from 40 crosses. Although he has not named any yet, Mike has made great improvements to the split-corona daffodils currently available and his seedlings frequently make it to the Premier table. With limited space he must be ruthless and quickly discards any that do not meet his high standards. When Mike's division 11s become available they will be very much in demand.

Denise McQuarrie, Motueka Valley

Denise lived for 49 years with her husband Neil in the rural Motueka Valley. In the early 1970s she sowed open-pollinated seed and when they flowered she was hooked. In her heyday she made about 100 crosses (in all divisions) per year and sowed about 3,000 seeds. Denise does not register seedlings until they have done well in other people's gardens and in almost 50 years she has only registered 33 cultivars, though her beds are full of numbered seedlings well worthy of naming. Among her favourites are 'Jenny's Joy' 1W-W and 'Greenhill Rata' 3W-YYR. She has many very good pinks but is now excited by a red/pink seedling from Mike Baxter's 'Lakeland Fair' × David Jackson's 'Danger Zone'.

Aaron Russ, Christchurch
One of our youngest members, Aaron Russ made his first crosses in 1993 and now makes up to 180 crosses each year, predominantly in divisions 1–4, resulting in 3,000 to 6,000 seeds. He is a very successful exhibitor and includes many of his own raising among his entries. Although he is yet to name any, his cultivars often make it to the top table and he has won Premiers in many different divisions with daffodils he has bred. Aaron represents the future of New Zealand daffodil breeding.

Malcolm Wheeler from Canterbury
Malcolm Wheeler has been hybridising since the 1990s and has a special interest in getting colour into miniatures. He makes from two to ten crosses each year and has succeeded very well with wee beauties such as 'Ninepins' 3W-YOO, 'Kakariki' 3W-O and 'Jealous Heart' 2W-GOO. In standard-sized division 5 he has registered the beautiful 'Sutherland Falls' 5W-W and 'Alice Falls' 5Y-Y. His 'Mount Tutoko' 1W-W is also a superb flower.

Colin Crotty and Gordon Coombes, South Canterbury
Colin Crotty ran the successful Pleasant Valley Daffodils for many years and stepson Gordon Coombes took over when he retired. Both have been prolific hybridisers and bred daffodils for exhibition and garden display. Colin's Y-Rs – 'Omeomy' 3Y-R, 'Fever Pitch'

2Y-R and more recently the lovely 'Colin's Gem' 1Y-R – are splendid. He bred some fine red/pinks, such as 'Neon Blaze' 2W-R, and a number of split-corona daffodils including the highly regarded 'Manuka Drive' 11aW-Y. Gordon's introductions include 'Paige' and 'Georgie Pie' – a must-have for intermediate enthusiasts and many fine standard-sized daffodils such as 'Valley Beacon' 2Y-R and 'Fleeting Glimpse' 2Y-YYR. Gordon and Colin continue to register new daffodils.

Alistair Davey from Timaru
Alistair Davey does about 15 crosses a year as well as planting open-pollinated seed. He has registered several intermediates and competes successfully with his seedlings under number. He is concentrating on intermediates, miniatures, and divisions 1–3, 9 and 11.

Conclusion
Though daffodil breeding is alive and well in New Zealand, most of the enthusiasts are an ageing group – at a guess the average age of current hybridisers is between 60 and 70 years, the oldest being in their eighties and the youngest perhaps in their forties. So, given that it takes four to five or even six years to see the results from seed sown this year, things look well for the next five years or so. However, with few younger ones on the scene, it's not hard to draw conclusions about the future of hybridising unless we can find, entice and persuade other young people to take up the baton and join Aaron Russ.

Graham J Phillips has been growing daffodils commercially for more than 50 years and has been awarded the American Daffodil Society Gold Medal. A senior judge in New Zealand, he enjoys going to international shows and conventions

Denise McQuarrie and her husband Neil grew daffodils for 49 years. Neil passed away last year. Denise is a keen hybridiser, a senior judge and a Vice-President of the National Daffodil Society of New Zealand

The Netherlands

Carlos van der Veek

Narcissus 'Thalia' (*all photos* **Carlos van der Veek**)

When talking about daffodil breeding in the Netherlands it would be inappropriate not to mention **Matthew Zandbergen**. Zandbergen has only three daffodil cultivars registered in his name, but he bred one of the most famous trumpet daffodils of all time – 'Dutch Master'. Matthew Zandbergen worked as a sales agent for M van Waveren & Son and clearly he had an important part in the firm's breeding success. Van Waveren introduced 99 Daffodils among them the grand 'Thalia' (pictured).

Zandbergen was an inspiration to daffodil people, not only in the Netherlands but also in the United Kingdom and in the USA. His passion for daffodils brought him into contact with hybridisers all over the world and the knowledge he gathered was used to encourage other daffodil breeders. He knew the daffodil hybridisers and supplied them with bulbs and knowledge as needed. He was also an important link between bulb growers and hybridisers in the Netherlands and abroad.

N. 'February Gold'

Large-scale Dutch hybridisers 1900–1970
- **De Graaf Bros** were the most productive daffodil breeders by far, registering over 400 cultivars until the early 1960s. Only 'February Gold' (pictured), 'Fortissimo' and 'Sempre Avanti' are still in commercial production.
- **JWA Lefeber** registered 271 cultivars, of which the most famous are 'Birma', 'Burning Heart', 'Dolly Mollinger', 'Flower Record', 'Lemon Beauty', 'Professor Einstein', 'Barrett Browning' and 'Bella Vista'. Lefeber downsized his activity from the 1970s. Eye-catching 'Gentle Giant' (1995) (pictured), one of his last introductions, is doing well in the industry.

N. 'Gentle Giant'

N. 'Little Beauty'

• **J Gerritsen & Son** are probably the most famous Dutch daffodil breeders, due mainly to the introduction of a wide variety of division 11 cultivars that put split-corona daffodils in the spotlight. Of his 127 registered division 11 cultivars, 'Apricot Whirl', 'Cassata', 'Changing Colors', 'Congress', 'Cum Laude', 'Love Call', 'Orangery', 'Palmares', 'Parisienne', 'Rainbow of Colors', 'Sailorman', 'Sunny Girlfriend' and 'Tricollet' are all still grown on a large scale in the Netherlands. He registered 215 cultivars in all, including beautiful miniatures such as 'Baby Moon', 'Fuco', 'Little Beauty' (pictured), 'Little Gem', 'New-Baby' and 'Topolino' and great standard-sized daffodils including 'Chinese Coral', 'Pimpernel' and 'Pink Parasol', which are still in production.
• **Konynenburg and Mark** bred 165 cultivars in the 1950s and 1960s including the world-famous 'Ice Follies', 'Manon Lescaut', 'Marieke' and 'Saint Patrick's Day'.
• Other prominent early 20th-century Dutch daffodil breeders who registered more than 100 cultivars are **G Lubbe & Sons**, breeder of 'Actaea' (pre-1919); **Warnaar and Co** whose 157 introductions included 'Aflame' (1938) and 'Golden Harvest' (1920); and **C G van Tubergen**, of which nine of his 100+ cultivars are still in production in reasonable numbers.
• Between 1920 and 1970, there were a lot of breeders who put a large stamp on the Dutch

daffodil industry including **A Frylink & Sons** (23), **G H Rotteveel & Sons** (20), **J J Grullemans & Sons** (40), **J H Rijkelijkhuizen** (9), **E H Krelage & Son** (40), **L van Leeuwen** (77), **P de Jager & Sons** (34), **P van Deursen** (79), **R A van der Schoot** (11), **P Th Zwetsloot** (16), **Walter J M Blom** (101) and **A C van der Schoot** (55).

Dutch hybridisers 1970–2000
By the last decades of the 20th century, only a handful of daffodil breeders were active.
• **W F Leenen** was an upcoming breeder who managed to bring some new flair to daffodils with cultivars such as 'Wild Carnival', 'Pistachio', 'Blues', 'Sagitta', 'Taurus' and 'Waltz'. Still operating today, the company now focuses more on viridiflora hybrids and daffodils for cut-flower production.
• **Mr Th van der Hulst** had great success with double daffodils including 'Ambon', 'Innovator' (syn. 'David Copperfield'), 'Flower Power' and 'Queen's Day'. In all he has registered 33 standard-sized division 4 daffodil cultivars.
• **D Van Buggunum** was a very successful small breeder in this period, and of his 11 daffodils, 'Las Vegas', 'Exception', 'Best Seller', 'Attraction' and 'Ballade' are grown commercially in decent numbers.
• **Karel van der Veek** started hybridising in the 1980s. A commercial agent specialising in daffodils, he had a huge collection behind his house to show growers and exporters what was available. Mr Gerritsen persuaded Karel van der Veek to start the collection after he showed Karel all his amazing new split-corona daffodils but told him it would be difficult to sell them if growers did not get to see them. Gerritsen lived in the Lisse area and because most daffodils were grown in the northern part of the Netherlands, it made sense to showcase them at Karel's house in the north so that local growers had easier access. It was such a success that W F Leenen and Wim Lemmers also planted their new cultivars in Karel's garden the following year.

His collection grew to more than 2,500 registered cultivars and in the late 1970s Karel and his son Carlos started hybridising, aiming to breed different bloodlines. Wim Lemmers and other growers brought cultivars from the USA, United Kingdom and New Zealand, which were crossed with Dutch daffodils. Over the years Karel registered 110 new daffodils and every year new ones are added as many Karel van der Veek seedlings under number remain with Dutch growers.

21st-century Dutch hybridisers

Only four daffodil hybridisers are currently active in the Netherlands.

• **Jan de Winter** and **Rinus van der Salm** are both retired bulb growers breeding smaller standard daffodils for garden and pot culture. Although called miniature in the Netherlands, this size of daffodil is too large for exhibition as a miniature at a daffodil show. Aiming for the size of 'February Gold', 'Jetfire' or 'Tête-à-tête', they are getting some good results. Jan's cultivars include 'Art Design', 'Iwona' and 'Lady Madonna' (pictured), while Rinus has bred 'Rataplan' (pictured), 'Maria' and 'Stef'.

Several growers have Winter and Van der Salm seedlings in production and we can expect many more things to come from them.

• **Arno Kroon** is a true daffodil enthusiast but operates a very commercial approach when selecting his seedlings. He sets his goals high; the seedling needs to show a good rate of increase and stay healthy without the use of chemicals. Naturally, the beauty of the flowers counts but if he has the option of a perfect flower and a lesser-looking one that increases rapidly and is healthy, he will pick the latter.

• **Carlos van der Veek** is continuing the work his father Karel started some 40 years ago. Together they bred on a large scale but when his father passed away in 2003, Carlos had his hands full, sorting and selecting the thousands of seedlings they had bred together with the vast collection of 2,635 named cultivars that needed to be looked after. In the past decade he has started again, focusing on garden daffodils. He is interested in show flowers but a daffodil that performs well with a lot of good-looking flowers that bloom well above the leaves is the perfect one for Carlos.

Conclusion

Enthusiastic breeding by previous generations in both the Netherlands and abroad has shown what can be achieved with the daffodil. It is truly amazing to see how flowers have changed over the past 100 years and it makes you wonder what will happen in the future. As hybridisers from all over world continue to exchange daffodils, I am curious to see what will be released from this immense gene pool.

Carlos van der Veek *is owner of Fluwel, Burgerbrug, and offers a wide range of bulbs for home gardeners at: webshopfluwel.com*

Modern-day introductions 'Lady Madonna' (above) and 'Rataplan' (right)

United States of America

Richard Ezell

The history of US daffodil breeding starts with **Mrs F Stuart Foote** of Battlecreek, Michigan, who registered daffodils from her crosses as early as 1888. Her graceful 'Firebird' can still be seen in the historic section of US shows.

Roberta Watrous, one of the founding mothers of the American Daffodil Society, discovered miniatures in the early 1940s and her tiny 'Flyaway' from around 1950 – still a charmer – was perhaps the first flower of Division 12 character to be registered.

There were others who helped expand interest in the daffodil, but the most important element in the history of US *Narcissus* work began with **Grant Mitsch** near the mid 20th century. Mitsch's first major success was 'Festivity' in 1954, a flower that dominated 'Best in Show' awards for years, but he registered close to 500 hybrids, working in all divisions, particularly the higher ones, and in spurring development of reverse bicolors such as 'Daydream'. His little 'Jetfire' 6Y-O is a worldwide favourite.

Mitsch's friend **Matthew Fowlds** concentrated on the higher divisions with considerable success: his miniature 'Chit Chat' AGM 7Y-Y and the triandrus hybrid 'Chipper' are still often seen.

Another friend, **Murray Evans**, is best known for 'Quasar' 2W-PPR, which figured prominently in development of near true-red in the coronas of white-petalled cultivars.

Amateurs have, almost from the beginning, played an important part in developing American daffodils, but none so important as **William (Bill) Pannill** who registered his first ones in 1970 and totalled more than 200 by

his death in 2014. One of his earliest, 'New Penny' 3Y-Y in 1972, is still by far the most often seen bloom of that classification in US shows and his 'Chromacolor' is grown by the acre in Holland. He worked with miniatures and all divisions of standards (except split-coronas, which he did not like).

Also very important was **Dr W A Bender**, an MD who, in addition to a number of outstanding originations, such as 'Conestoga' and 'Tuscarora', was internationally known for his knowledge of *Narcissus* pests and diseases.

No note of hybridisers, even those not well known through travel, publications or any sort of self-advancement, would be complete without mention of **Manuel Matos Lima**. Talk about single-mindedness: Manuel was devoted to green in daffodils – that and nothing else. Shy and solitary, Manuel worked only to breed the green of *N. viridiflorus* into any hybrid he could manage. Certainly not without aid: **Bob Spotts** went out of his way to assist, supplying materials and encouragement throughout his acquaintance with Lima, and after the hybridiser's death was, along with **Harold Koopowitz**, chiefly responsible for managing what he could of Manuel's heritage. Sadly, the first generation of Lima's greenies proved almost totally infertile. Koopowitz has produced a couple of hybrids using 'Lima's Green Success' 12G-GGO; I'd guess that bit of fertility is the reason Harold named it for its success when he registered it.

By far today's most prolific and impressive hybridiser is **Dr John Reed**, America's latest winner of the Peter Barr Memorial Cup, who has been known to make a single cross over a thousand times. His health now limits what he can do physically without help, but he is still after the perfect trumpet that he can colour-code W-O or W-R. He says 'Millennium Orange' 1W-O (pictured) is his closest yet, but he's still looking.

John is not the sort of person to limit himself; he has bred cultivars in every division and has a few miniatures. Among his best are 'American Cowboy' 2Y-R, 'Windy City' 1W-Y

John Reed's *N.* 'Millennium Orange' (*photo* **Kirby Fong**)

Bob Spotts' *N.* 'Mesa Verde' (*photo* **Tom Stettner**)

and 'Sherwood Poet', a miniature poeticus with a greenish perianth.

Californian breeders

Harold Koopowitz has done amazing work in Southern California in a more unforgiving climate than almost any other hybridiser. Harold has specialised as meticulously as John Reed and searched far and wide and into the wild in search of new breeding material.

He devotes himself chiefly to miniatures, especially those that bloom in the autumn or winter and to daffodils with more and more green coloration in perianth and corona. Few new introductions of modern hybrids have come close to causing the excitement in our world that his miniature Divison 11, 'Itsy Bitsy Splitsy', did in 2007. For those who can handle their growing requirements, Harold's many other introductions offer rewards in grace and uniqueness.

Another California hybridiser has created a comparable excitement to 'Itsy Bitsy Splitsy' – **Bob Spotts** with his 'Mesa Verde' 12G-GGY (pictured) in 2001 caused a similar near frenzy of interest and it still stands out as different and attractive. Spotts has ranged widely through the divisions, covering most. One introduction in particular has probably been more widely grown than any other cultivar bred in the US – 'Kokopelli' 7Y-Y, recently labelled in the British press as 'the ubiquitous 'Kokopelli''. And why not... it is cute and vigorous, a rapid multiplier. But wouldn't you know in the US is has been controversial ever since its introduction in 1993 – one of Bob's first releases. Is it a standard or a miniature? Hard to believe, but it still causes arguments over that question whenever shown.

Bob himself is unfazed, even seems to enjoy the hubbub. His opinion: "It's either... or both". When it grows big and with lots of blooms or largish ones it's a standard; otherwise it's a miniature. Who's so hard up for a controversy as to concern themselves? It's a much awarded all-rounder – RHS AM for exhibition (2001), RHS AGM (2004) and ADS Wister Award (2007) for garden worthiness.

Late 20th-century hybridisers

Among hybridisers whose work brightened the late 20th century years: **Eve Robertson**, whose 'Amy Linea' may no longer be available, but remains a beautiful 3W-GWW; **Helen Link**, whose 'Pogo' 3W-GYO, registered in 1989, is one of the most sought-after intermediates and, just a few months ago, won the coveted Pannill Award for most outstanding American show flower of the year; **Meg Yerger**'s sole aim seemed to be to promote poeticus hybrids and registered over a hundred of them; **Bill Welch** was almost as devoted to a single division and was known worldwide as 'the Tazetta Maven'.

Two other significant Californians: **Sid DuBose**, whose 'Brooke Ager' is still popular; and **Bill Roese**'s 'La Paloma' 3W-GYR (pictured) remains one of the most sought after of the many with that classification.

A bit farther north, Grant Mitsch's daughter **Eileen Frey** has specialised in miniatures: her 'Little Darling' 1Y-Y, which first bloomed in 1982, is still one of the best mini trumpets today.

Midwest breeders

In the Midwest, **Leone Lowe** is best known for her miniatures but her large 'Mississippi Traveler' 2W-Y looks to be one with staying power and miniature trumpet 'Roundita' is widely grown in Holland.

Much respected for her educational work with daffodils, **Mary Lou Gripshover** has

Bill Roese's *N.* 'La Paloma' (*photo* **Kirby Fong**)

hybridised several widely grown cultivars and 'Final Curtain' 3W-GYY is one of the best.

Brent Heath, who has carried on his family's lengthy association with the genus, has made 33 registrations to date. His 'Golden Echo' 7W-WYY is one of the world's best jonquil hybrids for gardens and showable as well. 'Snow Baby' is an excellent and vigorous little white trumpet now grown in quantity. **Daniel Bellinger**'s 35 registrations include several outstanding cultivars but none, sadly, seems to have achieved a wide appreciation.

South Central US hybridisers

In south-central US, **Larry Force** is one of our most interesting and promising hybridisers. Larry has registered only a handful of cultivars but his 'Strawberry Ruffles' 3W-YYR and numerous miniature hybrids seen in his show entries have us all looking forward to more.

Among daffodil folks, Force is one of a number of younger American hybridisers who are serious workers determined to produce new cultivars we'll all want to see and grow.

Michael Beringer in chilly Minnesota has only so far named half a dozen but is now planning on having more time for his work and he has lots of excellent material, much of it imported from Down-Under breeders.

Clay Higgins has now set himself up in a new, perhaps more propitious soil and climate situation and the few registrations he's made may be expected to be joined by many more.

True 'pro' **Mitch Carney** is knowledgeable, serious and willing to work extremely hard. His promising seedlings seem certain to soon provide us with improvements in a number of divisions and colour developments.

Northwest US breeders

Bill Carter, in the northwest corner of the US, is possibly the newest entrant into the hybridising arena. Bill has thrown himself into the game with tremendous enthusiasm, determination and energy (several hundred crosses this year) and is likely to eventually make his name and work known to all of us.

Conclusion

To finish this survey of American hybridisers, the true leader of them all, both now and looking into the future, is **Elise Havens**. With the passing of her father Grant Mitsch and then her husband and helpmate **Richard Havens**, the family business came to an end in 2014. Elise participated in several ways in helping to carry out many of the almost 800 daffodil introductions of the family, a good third of them pretty much solely hers, and with improved health and undiminished enthusiasm she's planning and hybridising. New and happy surprises are almost certain to appear before our eyes in the days to come.

As Elise Havens looks to the future so should we all: The American Daffodil Society is increasing its efforts to lure young potential gardeners under the spell of the *Narcissus* with gift memberships, bulb giveaways, mentoring programmes and special competitions. It seems relatively easy to capture the interest of youth; the problem is to maintain it.

The joys of daffodil hybridising are long lasting but rarely offer the instant gratification so often demanded today. Maturity may be a requirement; maturity will come and as it does the flowers will be there.

Richard Ezell *made his first daffodil cross in 1967. Maturity has come, but he's still waiting for that super bloom asleep in a seed pod picked last spring*

Summary

Brian S Duncan

Permitted only limited space, our contributors have nevertheless given excellent reviews of daffodil breeding activities in their respective countries. It seems that breeders are mostly well into retirement years and only a few may be considered as young at under 50 years of age. Efforts to encourage young people have not met with great success and contributors are less than optimistic about the future.

The graph below provides a statistical analysis of daffodil registrations worldwide in each decade since 1950. In that time a total of 18,744 names were registered, an average of 267 per year. This compares with an average of 241 per year in the last decade so there has not been much decline. However, if our contributors are correct in their assessments there may be a much steeper decline in future.

In the 1950s, 1960s and 1970s Australia was world leader, with 1,186, 947 and 728 registrations per decade respectively and about a dozen active breeders in the country. Since then far fewer people have been involved in Australia and now the other southern hemisphere country, New Zealand, where there are many current breeders, has taken over as leader in this league table.

Average number of registrations per year, per country, over past 70 years

Country	Average registrations/year
Australia	65
New Zealand	59
USA	47
England	36
Northern Ireland	27
The Netherlands	22
Republic of Ireland	8

Analysis such as this can never tell the whole story. The decline in the Republic of Ireland is almost entirely due to the demise of the House of Richardson. Had we taken in a couple of earlier decades then Scotland and Wales would have figured large through the efforts of The Brodie of Brodie and A M Wilson who registered 410 and 387 new names respectively.

With well over 30,000 names now in the *International Daffodil Register and Classified List* we might ask if we need many more daffodils. Comments over the years cause reflection – a Dutch breeder said "We certainly don't want any more yellow trumpets," and an American friend asked "Does the world really need any more 2W-Ps?" Once, when standing proudly in front of our exhibit of new pink doubles at an RHS show a passing lady sniffed to her friend "Why do they do that to daffodils?"

Looking to the future

So, where do we go from here? I think this review has pointed out trends for the future – there may be less people involved but specialisation will be key.

Already we see more interest in the development of miniature and intermediate daffodils, of viridiflorus hybrids and cultivars suitable for pot culture. Also, the pursuit of new perianth colours will continue, whether or not such flowers will ever enjoy public admiration.

ACKNOWLEDGEMENTS

The author is indebted to the contributors to this symposium who so willingly gave up their time to research and supply the background and up-to-date information about daffodil breeding activities in their respective countries.

I also wish to acknowledge the American Daffodil Society's daffseek.org. from which figures have been extracted for statistical information and to thank Peter Duncan and Lucy Giles for design of the graph.

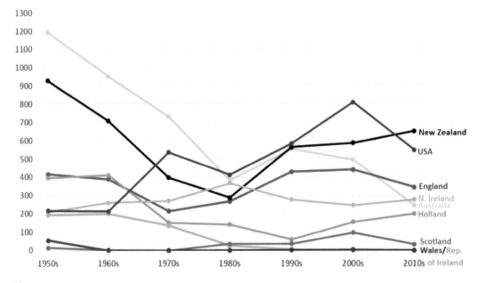

Worldwide daffodil registrations by decade since 1950

Division Three daffodils –
with a white perianth and orange or red predominant in the corona

John Gibson

We continue our annual progression through different daffodil categories. When asked to write this article, I was minded to restrict this year's discourse to cultivars registered with a solid red or orange corona, without any other colouring present. However, predominant flowers fall into two categories: those that have been registered with a single colour – either red or orange; and those that include a yellow or green eye zone. Several fine flowers fall into the second category that I feel must be included.

Over the past 20 years, 39 cultivars have been registered with a corona of a single uniform colour either red (18) or orange (21); a further 13 cultivars have been registered with red or orange predominant in the corona. Most of these cultivars I have not grown, nor even seen live specimens on the show bench; therefore in the main, I have made my comments and observations from photographs and information available on the American Daffodil Society's Daffseek database and also from entries in the RHS International Daffodil Register and Classified List.

I have to say, not all the available pictures

'Peter Ramsay' (*photo* Ron & Margaret Tyrrell)

show a strong resemblance to the registered details and I sometimes wondered if I was looking at the same flower. This may be due to flowers being grown in different geographical area from that of the originator, with varying growing and climatic conditions.

Show bench challenge
Having pristine blooms available for the show bench is a major challenge for hybridisers and exhibitors when growing this category of flower because the quality of the corona needs to be maintained. Coloured flowers are notably susceptible to burning of the cup, and therefore need shade and a cool atmosphere to develop to their best potential. It is not surprising, therefore, to find that this particular colour coding we are examining is one of the most difficult areas of daffodil breeding in which to achieve success; firstly, you need the flower to measure as a small-cup; which is usually only a low percentage of any batch of seedlings. Then, the occurrence of a corona with pure solid colour is uncommon; to combine these two qualities with a smooth white perianth and good healthy bulb that increases well is a rare event indeed.

'Doctor Hugh' (*photo* **Brian Duncan**)

'Bluntington' (*photo* **Michael Baxter**)

Early beginnings

In the great majority of cases, flowers from all the major breeders in both hemispheres can trace their pedigree back to that very important and prolific cross 'Kilworth' × 'Arbar'. Extracts from an interesting article in the 1970 Yearbook (pp27–32), analysing the cross made by Lionel Richardson at Waterford in Ireland, state the cross was used five times between 1949 and 1956, resulting in 2,400 seeds being sown, from which 38 flowers have been named. In my view the best of them turned out to be 'Rockall'; registered in 1955, it remained for many years the flower to beat and was still producing Best in Show blooms 30 years later.

Brian Duncan registered 'Doctor Hugh' (pictured) in 1975, which gradually took over the top spot; it is still the most widely grown and consistent exhibition flower in the category today.

John Lea's 'Cairntoul' registered in 1978 had its supporters, however, the depth of orange colouring was borderline as to whether it was predominant or not and visually it looked like a rimmed flower.

England

John Pearson contributed two cultivars in 2001 – 'Mount Ophir' 3W-R and larger 'Kuantan' 3W-R. Combined with better form in the perianth, it has been more successful in the single bloom classes with wins at several major United Kingdom shows.

Clive Postles bred several flowers in the mix. 'Ivanbrook' 3W-O, registered in 2015, has a deeply lobed cup, with overlapping lobes; the colour is a pale yellow-orange at the base, fusing into a stronger orange colour towards the edge of the corona. 'Tangerine Dream' 3W-O (2006), is a more triangular-shaped flower, with significantly narrower inner petals; a large pale yellow-orange eye zone dominates, with a darker-orange band at the edge of the corona. 'Lucy Scarlet' 3W-R (2010) has a stronger orange colour in the corona, while the predominant 'Bluntington' 3W-YOO (pictured) registered in 2005 has the deepest colour of them all, and perhaps is the most popular with exhibitors.

Two of John Blanchard's more recent raisings, 'Warmwell' (2004) and slightly later-flowering and larger 'Picket Post' (2005) both

'Spin Doctor' (*photo* **Brian Duncan**)

'The Fighting Mick' (*photo* **Nial Watson**)

W-O, are of good form with rounded petals and tidy cups. Both have the same vibrant strong orange colour throughout the cup.

Ron Scamp's 'Trecara' 3W-ORR (2001) has a very broad and well-overlapped, pure white perianth and neatly expanded dark red corona with a softer orange shade towards the centre.

Northern Ireland

Knowing the wide-spreading range of Brian Duncan's hybridising programme, registering more than 400 named cultivars since the turn of the century, I find it surprising to see only a solitary contribution from him in the shape of 'Spin Doctor' 3W-R (2005) (pictured). There is a good clean contrast between perianth and cup, with the dark even colour of the corona spreading deep into the throat of the flower.

Nial Watson has kept the flag flying for the province with three new introductions. 'Hot Date' 3W-O (2013) is a classy flower with a fine perianth and neat, deep orange cup. Early-flowering 'Ringhaddy Sunrise' (2017) is a very useful addition to this group. His latest, 'The Fighting Mick' (2018) (pictured), is a more triangular-shaped flower with narrower petals.

Nial also registered 'Fiona Linford' (2006), which has a noble poise, top notch perianth and neat, deep reddish-orange cup, raised by Sir Frank Harrison at Ballydorn Bulb Farm.

USA

In the USA, in exception to most other breeding lines, Dr John Reed has used what we call pink cultivars to increase depth of colour. He has raised a series of flowers all registered as 3W-R, 'Bristol Pink' (2002) (also marketed under the synonym 'Bristol Red'), 'Maraschino Cherry' (2007) and 'Red Wine' (2015).

Notes attached to the daffodil registration application form state: "In distinguishing Yellow from Orange in daffodil classification, borderline colours including and on the green side of RHS Yellow-Orange Group 15 are said to be Yellow; colours including and on the red side of Yellow-Orange Group 16 are Orange. In distinguishing Orange from Red in daffodil classification, borderline colours including and on the yellow side of RHS Orange Group 29 are said to be Orange; colours including and on the purple side of Orange-Red Group 30 are Red."

So we have a conundrum – sitting in the middle of the Orange-Red spectrum is the option for registrants to use a pink colour code. The registration documents also state: "It is at the registrant's discretion to distinguish Pink from the paler tones of Orange or Red". Given this pink breeding heritage, some would have registered these flowers in the pink spectrum; however, colour is defined by hue, brightness and saturation. John has intensified the saturation to produce some of the darkest red flowers around. In both 'Maraschino Cherry' and 'Red Wine' the colour intensifies as you move from the eye zone to the perimeter of the flattish cups.

'Mexican Hat' 3W-R (2007) bred by Bob Spotts, even if it is only 92mm (3½in) in size, has a superb sparkling perianth and colour contrast, making it a beautiful sophisticated flower, although its medium size would count against it for many British exhibitors.

Australia

'Afficionado' 3W-O (1997) with its very small, vivid orange disc-shaped corona, was raised by David Jackson and is still popular on the show bench. 'Abstruse' 3W-R (2005) has a stronger colour and appears to be much more refined.

New Zealand

Spud Brogdan's input into this area appears in the delightful form of 'Showdown' 3W-YOO (2007). It has a similarly shaped flower to its seed parent 'Centrefold' 3W-YYO with a predominantly orange corona. Spud's other contribution 'Fireonice' 3W-R (2009) has broad petals well overlapped, forming a super perianth, which is the perfect background for the flat disc of a corona. 'Seedalene' 3W-O (2012) from Graham Philips has a clean contrast between perianth and corona and with no trace of yellow staining.

In the South Island, Malcolm Wheeler has used N. *atlanticus* as the seed parent in raising three entries in this category, which are all single-flowered miniature daffodils. Firstly the cross using pollen from the 9W-R seedling

Q21-2-03 resulted in 'Tantalising' 3W-O (2008) with its pale yellow-orange corona. 'Ninepins' 3W-YYO (2014) followed, which notably achieved the accolade of Premier Vase of Miniatures at both the 2013 and 2017 South Island National Show. Malcolm's latest selection 'Kakariki' 3W-R (2019), winner of the best Miniature Single Stem when shown under its seedling number M95-H at the 2018 North Island National Show, looks to be a superb addition to the miniature stable. Both were bred using pollen from a McQuarrie 9W-R A42 seedling onto N. *atlanticus*.

Finally the colourful illustration of 'Peter Ramsay' 3W-YRR (2019) pictured here and on the front cover of the 2019 Yearbook is, in my opinion, the epitome of what a division three white-red flower should look like, featuring a pure white, spreading perianth combined with purity of the colour throughout the cup although, when I checked the registration details, it is registered with a yellow eye zone.

Conclusion

Although several excellent new cultivars have been introduced in recent years, further areas of work for the hybridist would be to improve the tidiness of the cups, as many are frilled or lobed, or both, to a greater or lesser extent. Other key targets are to achieve purity and intensity of colour in a single tone throughout the corona and, probably most important of all, developing a fully sun-proof flower.

Should anyone have the good fortune to breed such a flower, it is likely to be around for a very long time.

NOTES

The year of registration is given after a cultivar name. However, it will often have flowered as a seedling at least a decade earlier.

Narcissus Monograph project update

John David

Since the last update on the *Narcissus* Monograph project[1] it is good to be able to report on further progress and the fruition of plans previously mentioned. During the period we have produced two major papers, the first in October 2018, was the publication of the whole chloroplast genome of *Narcissus poeticus*, the type species of the genus[2]. This was the first time that the chloroplast genome had been sequenced for *Narcissus* and since then the team[3] have continued the work and we currently have sequences for 28 species.

These genomes can be used to look for new variable regions that could be of use to develop markers that might be effective in distinguishing cultivars using molecular methods. This work was announced at the international meeting Monocots VI, held in Brazil in October 2018.

The other publication is the main paper from Kálmán Könyves's PhD thesis on section Bulbocodii and appeared in July 2019[4]. Again, using molecular methods, the paper confirms previous published work on the genus in showing that the section as traditionally defined comprises two distinct lineages that appear to have evolved separately.

Section Bulbocodii is restricted to *N. bulbocodium* in its various forms and a new section, Meridionalis, has been created[5] for *N. cantabricus* (pictured), *N. romieuxii* and *N. hedraeanthus* (pictured). It also shows that the daffodil widely known as *N. cantabricus* subsp. *luteolentus* or *N. hedraeanthus* subsp. *luteolentus* is likely to be a hybrid between the two species. This should be known under the name *N. × blancoi* (pictured), published for this plant by Barra & López in 1992.

Narcissus hedraeanthus (*photo* **John David**)

N. cantabricus (*photo* **RHS/Phillipa Gibson**)

N. blancoi and hybrids (*photo* **Rafa Diez Dominguez**)

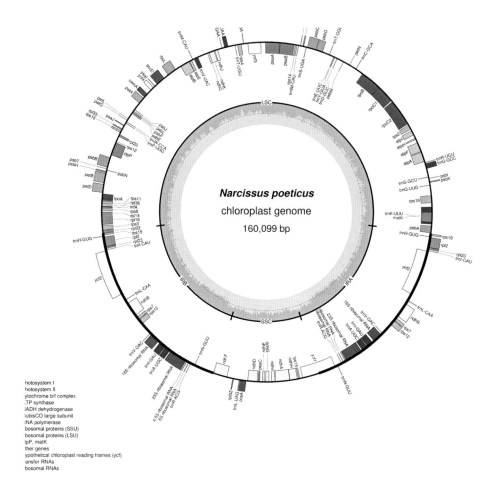

This circle represents the genetic code of the chloroplast genome for *Narcissus poeticus*. The 160,099 base pair code make up the genes that control photosynthesis and the transfer of energy around the plant cell, for instance, rbcL, an important gene for CO_2 fixation, is on the top left, coloured dark green.

Distinguishing the two sections morphologically is problematic, but in general Bulbocodii is characterised by being yellow-flowered and having a generally northern distribution in the Iberian Peninsula, whereas Meridionalis species have white, or pale creamy-yellow flowers and are found in the southern part of the Iberian Peninsula and Morocco. Yellow-flowered plants from southern Morocco will need further investigation to correctly place them in one of the sections. Additionally, *N. obesus* is recognised as a distinct species and this supports earlier chromosome work, which showed the species to have a base chromosome number of 13, in distinction to the rest of subgenus *Narcissus* that has a base number of 7.

PhD studentships

The research carried out as part of the *Narcissus* monograph project has been dependent upon a series of PhD studentships based at the University of Reading and part-funded by the RHS.

Jordan Bilsborrow, the second student, who studied the smaller-flowered trumpet daffodil species, submitted his thesis[6] in early 2019 and successfully passed his viva in July of that year. Since then he has been working on preparing papers from his thesis for publication.

We were successful in obtaining funding for a third studentship, which began in October 2019. The project is entitled Climate and speciation in the Mediterranean biome, but despite this it will concentrate on the evolution of *Narcissus* and use palaeoclimatic models to investigate the effect of climate on the evolution of the genus. The student, Zoe Dennehy, began last autumn and is already planning fieldwork in Spain and possibly in Morocco to cover gaps in sampling from the previous two studentships.

Collaboration

A third element to the project is a collaboration with Jerusalem Botanic Gardens. The Scientific Director, Dr Ori Fragman-Sapir, has been most helpful in providing samples of *Narcissus* from Israel, particularly *N. obsoletus*, the two kinds of *N. tazetta*, and the hybrid with *N. obsoletus*. This material is being sequenced, and will provide valuable data for the eastern end of the distribution of these species. We also plan to investigate whether there is a molecular basis for the difference between the autumn flowering upland populations of *N. tazetta* and the winter-early spring flowering valley populations.

Monograph

Plans for the monograph have progressed. The Alpine Garden Society, publishers of John Blanchard's book, have kindly agreed to collaborate with the RHS on a new book, based on John's original published in 1990. Preparatory work is under way but time to write it remains a challenge, as they say. What has been an enormous help are the various trips I have been invited to join, organised by Brian Duncan, to study the species and their hybrids in Spain. Not only has it provided an opportunity to obtain photographs but also gain an understanding of the plants which is not possible from herbarium material, or even when seen in cultivation.

John David *is Head of Horticultural Taxonomy at the RHS*

REFERENCES

[1] **David, JC** (2017) *Narcissus* monograph project. *Daffodil, Snowdrop and Tulip Yearbook* 2017: 74

[2] **Könyves, K, Bilsborrow, J, David, J & Culham, A** (2018) The complete chloroplast genome of *Narcissus poeticus* L. *Mitochondrial DNA Part B: Resources* 3(2): 1137–1138

[3] **Dr Alastair Culham** (University of Reading), **Dr Jordan Bilsborrow** (University of Reading), **Dr Kálmán Könyves** (Royal Horticultural Society), **Dr John David** (Royal Horticultural Society) and **Zoe Dennehy** (PhD student, University of Reading)

[4] **Könyves, K, David, JC & Culham, A** (2019) Jumping through the hoops: the challenges of daffodil classification. *Botanical Journal of the Linnean Society* 190(4): 389–404

[5] **Marques, I, Aguilar, JF, Martins-Louçao, MA, Moharrek, F & Feliner, GN** (2017) A three-genome five-gene comprehensive phylogeny of the bulbous genus *Narcissus* (*Amaryllidaceae*) challenges current classifications and reveals multiple hybridization events. *Taxon* 66(4): 832–854.

[6] **Bilsborrow, J** Towards a monograph in *Narcissus*; problems and challenges in the *N. minor* complex. PhD Thesis, University of Reading.

The story of *Galanthus* 'Wendy's Gold'

Bill Clark

I was engaged as Warden of Wandlebury Ring – an Iron Age fort within what is now a country park and nature reserve – in 1973. The following February I showed my wife a group of ten or so yellow-tinged snowdrops growing in the turf. Then, all we did was check their progress each spring until March 1985!

I heard a knock at the door and, apologising for being a nuisance, the lady explained that she had found what her son believed was a group of rare snowdrops in our grounds. She wondered if I would allow him to have one.

Her son was Joe Sharman, presently a horticultural student at what is now Writtle University College. Concerned about the loss of old garden cultivars, Joe searched in the vicinity of old houses and gardens for these now-uncommon plants and was especially keen on snowdrops. When we arrived at 'our' group of yellow-tinged snowdrops, Mrs Sharman asked how long I'd known about

them. "At least eleven years", I replied, and then, as I knelt to dig up a bulb, she exclaimed: "Bless my soul, there is my son coming over!" Joe arrived at my side saw the lumpy bulb with three flowers attached in my hand. Looking accusingly at me he said, "You knew they were here, and never did anything about them?"

I told him how I cared for Cambridgeshire's most loved parkland and was committed to restoring the chalk grassland with its wild flowers – so any now-naturalised flowers in the grassed-over gardens only held a cursory place in my interests. At least he could see I protected even those flowers from the public's picking and digging up.

"Joe", I said, "I think I have dug up what is about to become three bulbs. You can have them with pleasure, but only if you pay for them by letting me know everything you find out about them. Who knows? they may get a special place in my plant list after all!"

Five days later, I received Joe's payment! He had learned of a similar snowdrop in the 1920s in the Cambridge University Botanic Garden. Unfortunately all had been lost, probably during a botrytis epidemic in the 1940s, and the Wandlebury bulbs might be the only survivors but any name had been lost too!

He reckoned I should spend a couple of years bulking them up and we could probably sell them for at least £6 per bulb. "You ought to name them and they will need to be taken great care of – some collectors will go to any lengths to acquire one," Joe said. Indeed only a day or so later, I saw an elderly man diligently quartering the snowdrops so I dug up the bulbs and hid them by my house.

Commercial venture

At the next Cambridge Preservation Society, the owners of Wandlebury meeting, I spoke of my 'snowdrop problem' and suggested that we should sell them to a bulb-growing company. Instructed to go ahead I posted off a single flower, with an invitation to bid for 27 bulbs, to any firm that sold spring bulbs. Within days the Horticultural Marketing Arm of Geests was in touch and their Procurement Manager came to view the potted-up bulbs. "Caused quite a stir when I showed the flower to my colleagues," he commented!

I explained that one bulb was staying in the home where it had thrived for so long, Joe Sharman had three, and if ours successfully increased, we would give samples to RHS Garden Wisley and Cambridge University Botanic Garden. Finally, they were to be named 'Wendy's Gold' in honour of my wife, who had helped me so much during my years of looking after Wandlebury. He seemed quite happy with this, and made an offer of £250.

No other bids came, so when a disease expert arrived to examine the bulbs, gave an enthusiastic appraisal and mentioned that his boss had flown to Holland with the flower, I expressed my disappointment at the low price offered. A few days later a letter arrived from the Procurement Manager with three options: (1) £1,000 outright payment, (2) £250 with a five pence royalty per bulb over five years and (3) £500 with £500 worth of trees and shrubs for Wandlebury. Being a firm believer in the 'bird in the hand' theory, I accepted a £1,000 cheque for the Cambridge Preservation Society.

Sworn to secrecy

I was asked to keep it a secret from the gardening world, as they wanted to make a 'splash' – probably in spring 1988. With no evidence of a 'splash' by 1989, I phoned up, to be told, "Geests are no longer here, but we have taken over their business!" I was shuttled to various business offshoots – and finally to the original Procurement Manager.

He was very friendly until I asked about

Galanthus '**Wendy's Gold' – a snowdrop with a story to tell!** (*all photos* **Anne Wright**)

'Wendy's Gold' and he reluctantly told me: "We lost the lot in a fungus infection after the final chipping. The first was so successful that we didn't keep bankers"!

Successful partnership

Joe Sharman was by this time a partner in Monksilver Nursery and I had successfully cross-bred other snowdrops to hand over to him. The best was 'Wandlebury Ring' and an unflowered bulb, which he later named *G. plicatus* 'Bill Clark'! It was reputed that a single bulb of 'Wendy's Gold' changed hands for £70 in the early days, but the only buyer I met, in 1999, was a very happy lady from Australia who said she would have killed for one and had paid just £10.

Before I retired in 1998, one of the last tasks Wendy and I undertook was to plant a group of 'Wendy's Gold' back on the exact spot of the originals – but suffice to say, the occasional trowel hole still appears!

Bill Clark *retired after 25 years' service as Head Warden of the Cambridge Preservation Society but he and Wendy still live at Wandlebury Ring and keep an eye on the snowdrops. Bill is President of the Cambridge Beekeepers Association and an Honorary Member of several local societies*

Irish snowdrops

Paddy Tobin

Galanthus 'Cicely Hall' – the best Irish snowdrop – (above left) bears the name of the late snowdrop breeder of Primrose Hill, where 'Ruby Baker' (above right) was also found (*all photos* **Paddy Tobin**)

For this article I have selected what might be called 'the great and the good' of Irish snowdrops – those that are well-established, deeply loved and appreciated and reasonably readily available. I am not trying to present a comprehensive listing of Irish snowdrops, simply a selection of some favourites.

When first introduced in 1884, and considered an autumn-flowering form of the common snowdrop, *Galanthus rachelae* was a sensation. The bulbs I now grow under that name came from the garden of the late Primrose Warburg, through the kindness of two great snowdrop enthusiasts. Its history and connections with Sir John Pentland Mahaffy, Provost of Trinity College, and Frederick Burbidge, Director of the Trinity College Botanic Gardens, make a potful of them a snowdrop treasure in my eyes.

It was subsequently realised that it was a new species, *G. reginae-olgae*. Background and connections are what make snowdrops particularly special and it is an aspect I treasure very much. Such is the case with my selection of Irish snowdrops.

Primrose Hill snowdrops

The late Mrs Cicely Hall and now her son Robin, of Primrose Hill in Lucan, County Dublin, have played a pivotal role in Irish snowdrops. Snowdrops have always been given free rein in the ample grounds of Primrose Hill and nature, and careful selection, lead to many of what Mrs Hall would call 'Primrose Hill Specials'. However, she never applied this name to any particular snowdrop; it was simply her turn of phrase to describe a good seedling.

I will mention only two of the Primrose Hill snowdrops. That bearing Mrs Hall's name,

G. 'Cicely Hall' (pictured) is certainly the best of the Irish snowdrops –a strong-growing erect plant whose large flower has fully green inner segments of a deep rich colour, in the style of 'Merlin' and 'Robin Hood', but of greater substance and superior to both.

David and Ruby Baker were regular visitors to Primrose Hill and when Ruby admired an especially attractive seedling, Robin named it G. 'Ruby Baker' (pictured) for her. It appears to be a hybrid between *G. elwesii* and *G. gracilis* with an attractive rounded flower shape, a strong green basal mark to the inner segments and small marks on the nicely flared apices. I have treasured it in the years I have grown it.

Baker introductions

David and Ruby Baker introduced a number of excellent Irish cultivars. The late Dr Keith Lamb had spotted an attractive snowdrop in flower before Christmas, when visiting Sir George and Lady Mahon in Castlegar, County Galway in 1985. When David and Ruby visited Keith it caught their eye and they brought back bulbs to the United Kingdom. Enthusiasts considered it worth naming, particularly as it flowers reliably in early December, and Dr Lamb named it 'Castlegar' (pictured).

On another visit in 1995 they wandered off the beaten path somewhere in County Kildare, stopped at what looked like the remains of a gatehouse and found a derelict garden with several different snowdrops. They later named one fine tall snowdrop with green on the outer segments G. 'Kildare' (pictured). This large-flowered snowdrop is noticeably upright in habit and often produces a second scape. The outer segments are long and slim with thin green lines along the veins.

G. *elwesii* 'David Shackleton'

The story of the finding of G. 'Kildare' always brings a smile to my face, as does the naming of G. *elwesii* 'David Shackleton' (pictured). It was attributed to David Shackleton's fine garden, Beech Park, Clonsilla, County Dublin, and named for him, but he scoffed at the idea. Nonetheless, his name is now attached to an especially beautiful snowdrop that flowers late in the season, displaying pristine clear flowers that have an olive-green marking on the inner segment as well as a distinctly olive-green ovary. The whole plant, foliage and flower stalk, has an eye-catching upright habit.

British galanthophiles David and Ruby Baker introduced some excellent Irish cultivars including G. 'Castlegar' (above left) from County Galway and 'Kildare' (above right) from County Kildare

From top: *G. elwesii* 'David Shackleton',
'Straffan' and 'Hill Poe'

G. 'Straffan'

It was at Straffan House in County Kildare that G. 'Straffan' (pictured), often regarded as the champion of Irish snowdrops, arose. It is thought to be a cross between G. *plicatus* that Major Eyre Massey brought back from the Crimea and G. *nivalis* that was in the garden. Each bulb produces a secondary flower a little later than the first, significantly lengthening the display.

G. 'Straffan' has been with us such a long time, and passed around so many gardens, it is no wonder that other names have been attached to it over the years. Both 'Coolballintaggart' and 'The O'Mahony' are regarded as synonyms, though some would view them as separate.

G. 'Hill Poe'

G. 'Hill Poe' (pictured) was first noticed in 1911 in another of the old Anglo-Irish houses, Riverston, home of James Hill Poe in Nenagh, County Tipperary. This double snowdrop is a little jewel, usually with five outer segments and about 20 inner segments, perfectly regular, so neatly and tidily arranged. A late season flower, small in stature, it is certainly one of the finest double snowdrops and deserves to be placed in a choice position where it can be admired.

G. 'Greenfields'

Greenfields, also in County Tipperary, was the home of Mr W B Purefoy and, though the garden is now long gone, it was regarded as outstanding in its day. Liam Schofield was Head Gardener at Greenfields and took a special interest in snowdrops. He sent an especially good seedling of G. *nivalis* and G. *plicatus* parentage with a deep-green, large heart-shaped mark on the inner segment, to the National Botanic Gardens Glasnevin and to Brigadier L W H Matthias of the Giant Snowdrop Company and from there it came into general circulation as G. 'Greenfields'. I find it an especially good grower, healthy and reliable and wonderful in a good drift.

G. 'Emerald Isle'

Green-flushed G. 'Emerald Isle' (pictured) was found by Megan Morris at Drew's Court in County Limerick. A gently coloured flower, it is invariably admired by all who see it though the wish to grow it is a frustrating venture for some. The one bulb I received in 2002 increased slowly but has the compensation that, as a clonal variety, it comes true from seed. To rub salt into disappointed growers' wounds, it grows happily along 30m (98ft) of a field ditch in its original location, among brambles and nettles, trodden on by cattle and without the attention of any gardener.

G. 'Brenda Troyle'

It has been impossible to confirm the origins of G. 'Brenda Troyle' (pictured), though there is a general acceptance that it originated in Ireland and is perhaps connected with a Brenda Troyle who worked at Kilmacurragh in County Wicklow. Fairly similar in appearance to that great snowdrop 'S. Arnott', it gives a reliable and attractive display in the garden, being of good size and bulking up well.

It pains me that this short article does not allow a more comprehensive listing of Irish snowdrops for there are quite a number of other excellent cultivars: 'Green Lantern' and 'Skyward' from Altamont Gardens; 'Blaris', 'Waverley Aristocrat' and several others from Harold McBride; 'Pat Schofield', another of the Greenfields seedlings; 'Drummond's Giant' from the late Mrs Stasia O'Neill; 'Brocklamont Seedling' from Margaret Glynn in Ballymena; 'Lady Moore' given to me by a lady who received it from Lady Moore's hand; Angela Jupe's 'Jupe's Belle'; Emer Gallagher's 'Barnhill' and so on.

Connections! Provenance! The joy of snowdrops – and stories for another day!

Paddy Tobin *is an Irish galanthophile whose wife appointed him minder of snowdrops when the collection grew too big for her. For this he blames and thanks the unending generosity of snowdrop friends*

From top: G. 'Greenfields'; 'Emerald Isle' and 'Brenda Troyle'

New snowdrop findings in Slovenia

Jože Bavcon and Blanka Ravnjak

G. nivalis '**Green Dots' has light green dots on the inner segment tips (**all photos **Jože Bavcon)**

After many years of researching snowdrops in Slovenia, it might seem that nothing new and interesting is left to be discovered, but this is not true. Every season brings something new and it is always possible to discover another piece of land that reveals different information about *Galanthus nivalis*. Either novel morphological forms of plants appear, or we discover additional ecological rules for the species.

Quite a few new observations are certainly related to climate change. The past few years have been much warmer, which makes snowdrops shed their blossoms very quickly. However, despite the mild winters, the phenology of blooming remains more or less the same in individual parts of Slovenia (Bavcon 2014) and snowdrops do not start blooming sooner than they used to.

Phenology

Even in Slovenia, snowdrops begin blooming in the middle of winter, although they are considered the first heralds of spring. The latter is true for the central part of Slovenia. But the first snowdrops bloom in the second or even the first half of December in the Dragonja Valley [coastal region of Slovenia] (Bavcon 2014). However, even there, their blooming is stimulated by the cold. If there is no cold, they bloom around New Year.

Specimens collected in Dragonja retain the same blooming time in culture. In the Botanic Garden of the University of Ljubljana, where we keep a collection of over 6,300 pots of the common snowdrop, these specimens are the first to bloom. Their blooming is followed by specimens from Goriška, which bloom at the end of January despite the mild winters. They were already observed there in 1755 and 1761 by Wulfen (Wulfen 1858; Praprotnik 2016, Bavcon 2014), who wrote that they bloom at the end of January – their time of bloom is still the same (Bavcon 2014), and no more than a week earlier in really mild winters.

In cold winters with snow, they bloom at the same time. Some of the specimens have been in culture for 20 years, and they still retain their blooming time. This can be explained by the fact that these are genotypes that have adapted to the environment and are genetically fixed ecotypes. If they bloomed later in these environments, when the temperatures were already too high, their flowers would be scorched. However, they always need a cold period before they can start to bloom (Bavcon 2008, 2014).

On the mountain range overlooking the Gulf of Trieste, where the sub-Mediterranean and pre-Alpine climates meet, snow can persist until late April. Because of this, snowdrops still bloom towards the end of March and early April. These specimens retain this late blooming period in culture. Despite the past few mild winters, they still keep blooming in April in nature.

In the higher area of the same Dinaric-Alpine mountain barrier from 1,100 to 1,300m (3,610 to 4,265 ft), in the absence of snow, their blooming period gets very close to that of the specimens in the lower areas. In very cold winters with a few metres of snow and snowdrifts made by the Bora, a strong cold wind that blows along the Adriatic Coast, blooming extends as late as May.

Ecotypes and ecology

In all field research to date, we have found that certain morphological traits occur in a specific environment. In higher areas of the Dinaric-Alpine mountain barrier, specimens with very thick bulbs and broad leaves and robust flowers appear, which retain these characteristics in culture. In lower areas of the same chain between 900 to 1,000m (2,950-3,280ft), the mentioned ecotype occurs only where there are usually large snowdrifts. Where the thickness of the snow cover is normal, common snowdrops with normally broad leaves and flowers are present. The specificity of environmental conditions is most visible in mild winters with little snow.

When growing close to edges of snowdrifts, there are often populations with broad leaves and robust flowers. Pollen analysis showed that the populations with these characteristics were tetraploids (Paradiž et al 2018).

G. nivalis 'Blanka's Pearl' (above left) and 'Tris' (above right)

G. nivalis 'Kras' (above left) and *G. nivalis* 'Birth' (above right)

Another very interesting phenomenon are the snowdrops on long-term flooded Karst fields or intermittent lakes. In such locations, the common snowdrops reach only to the line of the highest floods, even though these occur only every 30 to 40 years. However, they do not spread below this belt. It is true, however, that snowdrops are often flooded along rivers, but these floods last for a maximum of two days. Because of this, they grow all the way to the normal river level. Here, occasional floods do not bother them. On intermittent lakes, snowdrops therefore stick to the highest water level, which is genetically recorded, while they do not let themselves be disturbed by rivers and streams, and allow themselves to be flooded. What is even more interesting is that snowdrops still linger on the banks of the former riverbed next to the ancient Roman port in Drnovo.

Green colouration

The third characteristic we have observed is that snowdrops along rivers and in flood zones more often have green stripes on their outer perianth segments or completely green-coloured outer perianth segments. With several consecutive annual floods, the frequency of such genotypes increases. According to several years of studies, these specimens are also stable. Similarly, we find that specimens belonging to the inverse poculiform group of plants are more common in locations where cold air intrusions or frosts are frequent. There, the frequency of this genotype is higher. Field findings have shown that in populations in which we have so far found special features within the species *G. nivalis*, new special features occur again.

We can conclude that these are very dynamic populations with a lot of genetic variability, where a certain type of special feature occurs over and over again. However, other populations remain fairly homogeneous for more than a decade after the collection of special specimens, and a similar special feature no longer occurs there. Such an example is *G. nivalis* 'Zvezdica' of the star type, which no longer appears in the population where it was first found.

In studies conducted in recent years, we have also found that some aberrations in individual specimens can also be the result of field spraying. Years ago, when we started researching these populations, there was never an aberration characteristic of some other populations. In the past seven years, with the start of cultivation of wheat fields, a very high frequency of individual special features appeared this year for the first time, such as different types of tufted specimens above the fertile head. This year, the frequency of these types was very common.

Novelty cultivars

The following are a few of the novelties in the snowdrop collection of the Botanic Garden of the University of Ljubljana biotechnical faculty.

• *G. nivalis* 'Blanka's Pearl' (pictured) is a member of the Poculiform Group and has up to nine semi-circularly rounded perianth segments in the form of a very rounded flower. At the suggestion of Matt Bishop, on a joint excursion around Slovenia, it is named after the finder.

• *G. nivalis* 'Tris' (pictured) is a form that occurs in only one location in Slovenia. It is characterised by having three flowers on a single flower stalk with incompletely differentiated pedicels. The first such occurrence was observed before 2008, and then it appeared every so often in some places. It does not bloom every year in culture; the specimen is the same as in nature only every few years.

• *G. nivalis* 'Green Dots' (pictured) is a variety of the Poculiform Group, which has very widely spread perianth segments. The inner segments are only slightly shorter and have light green dots on their tips.

• *G. nivalis* 'Kras' (pictured) is a variety with green-coloured inner segments with a white margin, which transition to completely white in their basal quarter. Its outer segments have long yellow-green stripes, which are most pronounced towards the apex.

• *G. nivalis* 'Birth' (pictured) looks as if it has one flower growing from another due to quite a number of petaloid bracts inserted in a cluster on the pedicel.

• *G. nivalis* 'Green Finger' (pictured) is a variety of the Poculiform Group. It has very narrow perianth segments, which have a green colour up to half of their length or more.

• *G. nivalis* 'Olive Patch' (pictured) has a simple olive-green pattern on its inner segments, which reaches up to a third of the segment and ends with a straight line. On the widest part of the outer segments, there are large olive-green spots, which transition into white at the tips and in the upper part.

G. nivalis 'Green Finger' (above left) and *G. nivalis* 'Olive Patch' (above right)

REFERENCES

Bavcon J (2008) Navadni mali zvonček (*Galanthus nivalis* L.) in njegova raznolikost v Sloveniji = Common snowdrop (*Galanthus nivalis* L.) and its diversity in Slovenia. *Ljubljana: Biotehniška fakulteta, Oddelek za biologijo*, 94pp

Bavcon J (2014) Navadni mali zvončki (*Galanthus nivalis* L.) v Sloveniji = Common snowdrop (*Galanthus nivalis* L.) in Slovenia. *Ljubljana: Biotehniška fakulteta, Oddelek za biologijo*, 308pp

Paradiž J, Bavcon J, Ravnjak B (2018) New advances in the use of PGD biomonitoring for *Galanthus nivalis* L. cytogenome diversity assessment. V: Baebler, Špela (ur.), et al. 7th Slovenian Symposium on Plant Biology with International Participation, Biotechnical Faculty, University of Ljubljana, September 17–18, 2018, Ljubljana, Slovenia. 1st electronic ed. Ljubljana: Silva Slovenica Publishing Centre, Slovenian Foresty Institute

Praprotnik N (2016) Seznam praprotnic in semenk ter njihova nahajališča na Slovenskem v delih Franca Ksaverja Wulfena = The list of vascular plants and their localities in Slovenia cited in the works of Franc Ksaver Wulfen. *Scopolia: glasilo Prirodoslovnega muzeja Slovenije.* No. 86: 1–143

Wulfen FX (Ed Fenzel E, Graf R) (1858) Franz Xaver Freiherrn von Wulfen's Flora Norica Phanerogama. *Im Auftrage des Zoologisch-botanischen Vereines in Wien.* 816pp (Note: Published long after Wulfen's death on 16 March 1805)

Dr Jože Bavcon has written extensively about snowdrops and is Director of the University of Ljubljana Botanic Garden. He was the 2015 recipient of the Marsh Award for international plant conservation

Dr Blanka Ravnjak *is a researcher at the University of Ljubljana Botanic Garden*

Snowdrop season 2020

G. 'Schorbuser Irrlicht' (*photo* **Matt Bishop**)

ULTIMATE SNOWDROP SALE
Mick Martin

I always look upon the Ultimate Snowdrop Sale as the harbinger of the spring snowdrop season. The first major event of the season took place at Myddleton House on Saturday 25 January. On arrival there were plenty of excited prospective purchasers already queueing, although it must be said not as many as previous years. From the outset it was noticeable that the sale was missing several of our regular European visitors.

For continuity the selling tables were set out in their usual positions, however this year without the 'Glen Chantry' stand (Sue and Wol Staines). Unfortunately, Wol was still recuperating from a recent health issue. A knock-on effect of their absence was the unavailability of the famous 'Chantry' flyer. This pre-sale flyer, setting out the snowdrop availability, is usually distributed to attendees standing in the chilly, early morning queue and is always a popular read before the sale.

Snowdrops of note
The following snowdrops were new to me:

Matt Bishop Snowdrops
• *G. gracilis* 'Andrea's Fault' is a fine large-flowered virescent, the outer segment veins conspicuously green-striped, inner segments entirely green except for the margin; introduction by Andy Byfield.
• *G.* 'Schorbuser Irrlicht' (pictured) – a first offering in the United Kingdom of this exciting colour-change yellow, a selection by well-known German collector and introducer of some mouth-watering cultivars, Hagen

Engelmann. Early flowering and with a bright yellow inner marking that covers most of the length of the inner segments, it is believed to have resulted from complex hybridity involving *G. nivalis*, *G. gracilis* and *G. plicatus*.

Monksilver Nursery (**Joe Sharman**)
• 'Ice Princess' is the first of a series of double-flowered poculiform *G.* × *valentinei* raised by crossing *G. nivalis* var. *pleniflorus* on to *G. plicatus* 'E.A. Bowles'. It was priced at £500 and raised from the only seed that resulted from the cross, which, not surprisingly, has been repeated.
• *G. elwesii* 'Anglesey Adder' was found at Anglesey Abbey in the early years of this century. It has a huge 'Scharlockii' style split spathe, though not the associated apical green outer segment markings, and it makes a fine tall plant.

Rainbow Farm Snowdrops
(**Michael and Anne Broadhurst**)
• *G. elwesii* 'Rainbow Yo-yo' is a robust cultivar and remarkably long-pedicelled selection (a monostictus).
• *G.* × *valentinei* 'Rainbow's End' a colour-change yellow offered for the first time.

G. plicatus 'Party Dress' (*photo* **Richard Bashford**)

Woodchippings
(**Richard Bashford and Valerie Bexley**)
• *G. plicatus* 'Party Dress' (pictured) is an elegant new inverse poculiform with noticeably striated single-marked outer segments and mostly green inners that often has two scapes.

SNOWDROP GALA AND OTHER SPRING TREASURES
Hester Forde

The annual Snowdrop Gala and Other Spring Treasures event was held in Carlow, Ireland on 1 February 2020. Now in its ninth year, the Gala has gone from strength to strength, attracting lots of visitors from overseas, including Austria and Germany this year. The Gala was born out of a love for *Galanthus* by Robert Miller and Hester Forde, who wanted to share their enthusiasm with like-minded people. Lectures each year take place at Mount Wolseley Hotel, now extending over the weekend and including an after-dinner talk on the Friday night.

Of the two lectures held on the Saturday, one is for the snowdrop enthusiast and the second covers the winter–spring garden but including snowdrops. This is followed by lunch and then a visit to Altamont Gardens to the plant sale, guided tour of the snowdrop collection and afternoon tea.

The Gala has had its share of noted speakers over the years including Alan Street, John Grimshaw, Graham Gough, Jim Jermyn, John Massey, Ian Young, Rod Leeds, Colin Crosbie, Richard Hobbs, Jim Almond, Ian Christie, Julian Sutton, Kevin Hughes and Jennifer Harmer.

The weather was glorious this year and speakers were Catherine Erskine on 'The restoration of Cambo Stables and Gardens fuelled by snowdrops' and Ross Barbour and Helen Picton of Old Court Nurseries and The Picton Gardens lecturing on 'Snowdrops need friends too'. Catherine gave the fascinating history of Cambo, the superb collection that now grows there, in particular *G.* 'Bloomer', *G.* 'Green Arrow' and *G. elwesii* 'Howard Wheeler', to mention just a few.

Ross and Helen gave us our first dual lecture, which was a treat, providing a great insight into how the woodland garden and winter garden began. They talked about how to create structure from the trees to the shrubs to the ground layer and the wonderful tapestry you can create overall. Snowdrops that stood out were *G.* 'Rodmarton Regulus' and *G. woronowii* 'Cider with Rosie'.

The afternoon sales are a highlight and present this year were: Altamont Plant Sales, Coosheen Plants (dwarf narcissus, snowdrops and spring bulbs) and Avon Bulbs showing and selling beauties such as *G.* 'Veronica Cross' and *G.* 'Pieces of Eight'.

Old Court Nurseries had a diverse selection of snowdrops with some wonderful *Iris unguicularis* selections and Cambo Estate had a delightful selection all beautifully displayed.

• Next year is our tenth anniversary and the event will take place on 6 February 2021 with speakers including Alan Street of Avon Bulbs and Tom Coward, head gardener at Gravetye Manor. See www.hesterfordegarden.com for further details.

AGS SNOWDROP STUDY DAY
Rod Leeds

The Alpine Garden Society held its annual Snowdrop day on 2 February at the Lilleshall Sports Centre near Telford.

There were three lectures given by doyens of the bulb world. In the first, 'Waves of Colour', Ian Young spoke on winter in Aberdeen where snowdrops have to earn their place in his intensively planted garden. Here bulbs are encouraged to seed to form drifts of colour, layer upon layer, as each season evolves. His garden and style of growing is well illustrated in his renowned Bulb Log.

Next was Joe Sharman of Monksilver Nursery, who has been breeding snowdrops for many years. He deliberately hand pollinates his chosen snowdrops and grows the resulting bulbs in deep boxes. He showed us many of his successes including G. *plicatus* 'Golden Fleece', the first all-yellow pterugiform (or inverse poculiform). He also spoke of future aims in developing the character of snowdrops.

The third speaker, renowned galanthophile and breeder Matt Bishop, talked about his analysis for the potential development of all attributes that could be bred into snowdrops. He showed what had been achieved and outlined a tempting range of possibilities.

Finally there was a question and answer session with all three speakers taking part.

Snowdrops on display

There was a display in the AGS fashion of potted snowdrops, with David and Margaret McLennan, holders of the Scientific National Collection of Snowdrops, exhibiting the latest two selections in The Dryad Gold series – G. 'Sceptre' and G. 'Standard'. Roger Norman

of Ivycroft Plants had a magnificent pan of G. 'Ivington Green', quite the largest inverse poculiform in circulation. G. 'Emerald Hughes', G. 'Green Genes' and G. 'Moya's Green' were also shown.

This indoor display always provokes considerable interest when there is time to look closely at the flowers. The large hall easily catered for the five nurseries and the 120 attendees.

SHAFTESBURY SNOWDROP FESTIVAL
Mick Martin

Now firmly ensconced on the annual snowdrop calendar, the Shaftesbury Snowdrop Festival took place on Saturday 8 February in the Arts Centre (for registration, lectures and refreshments) followed by the Guildhall (for plant sales).

From the start there was a distinct buzz around the packed auditorium in anticipation of the three distinguished speakers who were due to appear throughout the day's events.

The morning lectures commenced with Dr Aaron Davis, Senior Research Leader at the Royal Botanic Gardens, Kew. Within his comprehensive talk entitled 'Discovering and understanding snowdrop species, past and present', Aaron described his fascinating visit to Turkey last year when he visited the area where the newly-identified species, *Galanthus bursanus* had been found. Following news of the discovery, the new species was heralded in the columns of garden magazines and discussed at length on social media[1].

The second speaker was snowdrop expert Matt Bishop talking on 'Snowdrop potential... and potential snowdrops'. With the aid of excellent photographic images, Matt structured his talk around a detailed spreadsheet that looked at all possible combinations of a designated list of mutant phenotypes with examples of what already existed versus what was still to come in the evolution of snowdrops through controlled breeding. This system could well become de rigueur for galanthophiles in the future.

During the lunch break most delegates opted for the straight 'rush' to the nearby Guildhall for the exclusive VIP entry plant sale. They were not disappointed for choice because the usual sellers were primed ready, although unfortunately, two stalwart sellers, Wol Staines and Melvyn Jope, were both still recuperating from recent health problems. Sellers reported a brisk trade in new cultivars and the usual classic favourites. There was even a second surge of prospective purchasers when the general public were let in the hall following the exclusive VIP hour for delegates who had attended the lectures.

Snowdrops of note

Notable cultivars on display included, from Joe Sharman's Monksilver Nursery, a hybrid named G. 'Dirty Dishes' from the garden of Richard Nutt, which he sent Joe on account of its extraordinary orange colouration of the spathe membrane.

Woodpeckers, in the guise of Richard Bashford and Valerie Bexley, showed some excellent plants. They had a number of incredible pots of *G. × valentinei* 'Celia's Double' (pictured), which occurred in the garden of Celia and Walter Sawyer close to the presumed seed parent, *G. plicatus* 'Diggory'. In this instance 'Diggory' has passed on the extremely broad outer segments and, happily,

G. × valentinei 'Celia's Double' (*photo* Matt Bishop)

the incidence of a second much shorter scape so that the flowers are produced in two distinct tiers. Extremely vigorous, the flowers are regular in their arrangement with separate apical and basal inner segment markings and renowned textured outer segments.

Meanwhile Matt Bishop Snowdrops displayed two superb snowdrops within his selection. *G. gracilis* 'Tall, Dark and Handsome' from Andy Byfield offers a wonderful contrast between the coldness of the pure white segments to the depth of green of the crisp inner segment marking found in this robust tall plant. Brought along for interest was 'Lamplighter', a superb colour-change yellow hybrid of *G. rizehensis* and *G. nivalis* (the putative colour-change parent). The hybrid had green, widely splayed foliage with a discernible central stripe and two scapes with large flowers, cream segments at first, with a pale yellow single apical inner segment marking. Much drooling!

Afternoon events

In the afternoon session in the Arts Centre an Ask the Experts forum was led by three snowdrop experts – Dr Aaron Davis, Matt Bishop and Dr John Grimshaw, who collaborated in the writing of *Snowdrops: A Monograph of Cultivated Galanthus* (2001).

Dr John Grimshaw, Director of the Yorkshire Arboretum, and a renowned botanist and author then gave an interesting talk on 'Woody Plants for the Winter Garden' – a subject close to his heart. The day culminated in a self-guided tour of Old Rectory Garden at East Orchard, Shaftesbury.
● The Shaftesbury Snowdrop Festival is a very well organised event that is now firmly ensconced in the snowdrop annual calendar. Long may it remain so. For 2021 dates visit: https://shaftesburysnowdrops.org

REFERENCE

1. **Anon (2019)** New snowdrop found on Facebook. *Daffodil, Snowdrop and Tulip Yearbook 2019* 52

SCHNEEGLÖCKCHENTAGE KNECHTSTEDEN

Janet Benjafield

On 15-16 February, Knechtsteden Monastery hosted its second Snowdrop Days event. Marlu Waldorf, widow of the Nettetal originator Günter Waldorf, honoured the new venue with an emotional visit.

Although not the only plants to be offered here, snowdrops certainly seem to be the main incentive for many who visit, with large numbers of keen and knowledgeable collectors arriving early to form extensive queues at the gate before the rush to the sales tables.

Once again we were blessed with kind weather and temperatures, although Saturday night brought high winds that resulted in an early morning game of hunt the gazebo and overturned pots and tables as well as impacting on attendance. Even so, despite a poor forecast, 3,154 people attended over the weekend.

G. gracilis 'Belisha Beacon' (*photo* Janet Benjafield)

Snowdrops of note

Avon Bulbs had a great variety on offer with some notable new introductions including, for the first time here, *G. plicatus* 'Grumpy's Brother' from Mrs Elkington near Salisbury and *G.* 'Miss Prissy', a hybrid double bred from *G. nivalis* and *G. elwesii* and registered by Stephen Jackson. Also to be seen was *G. nivalis* 'Héloïse des Essourts', a double *G. nivalis* that was discovered by Jean-Pierre Panier in Normandy and named after his younger daughter.

Avon Bulbs also had an intriguing display of a wide variety of *Galanthus* flowers pushed through a hessian backdrop into hidden vases to make a large living picture. With cultivar names for comparison it easily disproved the commonly-held belief that all snowdrops look the same and gained a lot of interest from both Galanthophiles and non-followers alike.

Monksilver Nursery had a huge range of snowdrops on offer. For the first time they had *G. woronowii* 'Benjy's Baby' whose exceptionally large flowers for this species make it highly garden worthy. Another offering was *G. plicatus* 'Bowles Gemini', a first fully poculiform

snowdrop with two flowers per stem.

A new introduction for 2020 and causing quite a stir at the tables and on social media was *G. gracilis* 'Belisha Beacon' (pictured), a large sturdy flower on a strong scape, that had two dark green flat-topped marks either side of a deep sinus notch, with lighter green squared basal mark. The flower has a strong all-over deep orange shade on both outers and inners.

Lectures

Lectures given on both days proved popular. Volker Atrops spoke about 'New hope for boxwood', Michael Dreisvogt discussed 'Notable varieties of snowdrops' including advice regarding general cultivation conditions so that they thrive in the garden for many years, and Christoph Laade considered 'The garden treasures of the Cotswolds in England' that included plants, landscape and architectural design as well as snowdrops. Sunday lectures were accompanied by harpist Christine Högl as a 'musical snowdrop'.

● Next year's Knechtsteden will be held on 20-21 February 2021.

THE COTTAGE GARDEN SOCIETY SNOWDROP GROUP 2020
Mick Martin

The Cottage Garden Society Snowdrop Group ventured north to Harrogate Grammar School, North Yorkshire, for their Members' Day on Saturday 22 February. The school's excellent purpose-built lecture theatre was utilised for both the talks and plant sales. Unfortunately, it was again disappointing that more members did not attend the excellent programme of talks, gardens to visit and popular plant sale.

The first speaker, galanthophile Michael Myers, ventured into the rather complicated world of inverse poculiform and poculiform snowdrops including their characteristics and classification. Michael explained the fine nuances on the subject, which gave an insight into the differentiation there is between the many new snowdrop cultivars now available.

Our second speaker was botanist, author and galanthophile Dr John Grimshaw, whose well-documented talk, 'Six centuries of botanical illustration', included many varied slides covering botanical plates from early drawings to the more ornate, detailed coloured plates. Thankfully, the love of botanical illustration hasn't waned over the centuries.

Visitors then had the chance to visit Dryad Nursery, home of Anne Wright's snowdrop collection. Anne is known for her yellow snowdrops marketed under the 'Dryad Gold' label and her miniature daffodils. The magnificent garden was covered in swathes of self-seeded cyclamen that were stunning. The greenhouses and cold frames were the focus of her nursery for propagating new varieties of snowdrops, miniature daffodils and hepaticas.

The second garden was Fair View, home of Michael Myers, which was in complete contrast to the previous garden. The house and garden were located on the side of a steep hillside covering 0.2 hectares (1/2 acre). The garden had been landscaped into rocky outcrops with terracing with integrated footpaths leading around the garden. The tiered layout allowed it to contain many plants and shrubs located within sheltered beds. A large well-stocked alpine house set above the house contained lovely pots of snowdrops. A welcoming cup of tea and cake awaited visitors to the garden kindly served by members of Michael's family.

HPS GALANTHUS GROUP AGM & STUDY DAY
Eddie Roberts

The Hardy Plant Society Galanthus Group study day on Sunday 16 February, at Tuxford Academy Nottinghamshire was a success, despite the effects of Storm Dennis.

Following a well-supported plant sale, Mark Brown spoke about French snowdrops. Mark first told us the secrets of the famous Rosey Bank, in Normandy, and the chance finding of exquisite yellow G. nivalis 'Ecusson d'Or'. Sadly this woodland, that has been the source of so many interesting snowdrops, is about to be lost to a housing development. He then explained the difference between the Normandy colonies of G. nivalis, which are mainly seeding colonies and those in the United Kingdom, which are mostly clonal.

Anne Repnow then spoke about 'Galanthus galore, six months of flowering snowdrops in a German garden'. Ann's garden was stunning, with a superb collection of snowdrops, all of which she had photographed beautifully. As she described snowdrop after snowdrop my wish list expanded dramatically.

After lunch, despite the storm, there were two visits where we could see snowdrops in a garden context. At Church Farm, West Drayton near Retford, home of Bob and Isobel Adams, I noted an enclosed walled area where a superb collection of snowdrops, mostly in raised beds, were easy to admire and photograph. The second visit was to home of Margaret and Jean Swindon at The Beeches, Milton near Retford, where a wall on the right hand side of the drive, contained a narrow border along the top that was planted with interesting snowdrops. There were also easy to see and enjoy at eye level.

Abstracted with permission from the
HPS *Galanthus Group Newsletter*, Spring 2020

SCHNEEGLÖCKCHENTAGE IM LUISENPARK MANNHEIM

Janet Benjafield

Now in their 5th year, the Luisenpark Snowdrop Days were started by the indomitable Anne Repnow. This year they were held on 22-23 February and had a record weekend attendance of about 3,100.

Snowdrops of note

Avon Bulbs offered a superb snowdrop range with some enticing first-time offerings, including another German named 'drop that folks may struggle with pronouncing, *G. nivalis* 'Federschwingen' ('Spring Swing' in English) that was found by Kurt Kleisa.

Also available was Irish *G. plicatus* 'Green Lantern', which, when naming it, Paul Cutler of Altamont Gardens, County Carlow, had originally wished to link it to Mrs Corona North, owner of the garden but soon realised that it wasn't to be because so many other plants carried her name. *G. plicatus* 'Joe Sharman' was also on offer – a vigorous and prolific grower, and the only fully virescent form of subsp. *byzantinus*.

Monksilver Nursery had a large sales table with plenty of choice for all pocket sizes. Among Joe Sharman's offerings were *G. nivalis* 'Widder', a scharlockii with 'ears' that spiral dramatically with age like a ram's horn and *G.* 'Dirty Dishes', a vigorous hybrid with an orange spathe valve, white flower and curious in-rolled leaves. Also offered for the first time was tiny *G. nivalis* 'Big Lady' with disproportionately large flowers, from the late Günter Waldorf.

Lectures

Lectures were given from the raised stage area during the sales. Saturday saw Horst Bäuerlein of Bäuerleins Grüne Stube talk on 'Our native snowdrop, *Galanthus nivalis*, at the natural site'. On Sunday Iris Ney spoke on 'Lively gardens in winter' with Anne Repnow interviewed by Ellen Oswald on 'Snowdrops for everyone!'.

• Next year's Luisenpark Snowdrop Days are planned for 27–28 February 2021.

From top: *G. nivalis* 'Federshwingen' (*photo* Matt Bishop); *G. plicatus* 'Green Lantern' (*photo* Matt Bishop); *G. plicatus* subsp. *byzantinus* 'Joe Sharman' (*photo* Chris Ireland-Jones)

Cultivating species tulips for exhibition and in the garden

Mike Hopkins

Once established, tall *Tulipa sprengeri* pops up in all corners of the garden (*photo* **Mike Hopkins**)

In my previous article[1] I described my approach to cultivating species tulips destined for the showbench. I always use standard clay pots, packing my bulbs close together in the bottom third of the pot, which is then filled with compost to about 2½cm (1in) below the rim. I top up with a thin covering of grit, leaving about 18mm (¾in) to allow room to add more grit later for extra stem support and a clean cover for exhibition.

I have revised my compost mix frequently over the years, eventually settling on 50 per cent John Innes No. 2 and 50 per cent grit, plus leafmould at about a third by volume with a dash of bonemeal and sulphate of potash.

Bearing in mind the wide range of habitats and soils in which tulips thrive in the wild, I've come round to the view that good drainage and sufficient nutrients are key.

My cold frame is fairly remote from the main garden, so seeding down is not an issue. *T. sprengeri*, *T. tarda* and *T. sylvestris* spread their seed liberally in the open but no other species have arrived. We tend not to have summer rains on the Scottish east coast, so we don't need to dig our tulip bulbs up and dry them off to prevent rot.

I now take a closer look at my experience with growing individual species in pots and in the open garden.

Tulipa subgenus Clusianae
T. linifolia

The name *T. linifolia* (Batalinii Group) AGM (pictured) is reserved for the yellow-flowered forms. Previously the name *T. batalinii* has been used for the yellow form of *T. linifolia*. It has small, wine-glass flowers and upright pale-green leaves. Garden-worthy hybrids include 'Bronze Charm', 'Apricot Jewel' and 'Bright Gem' with 'Red Hunter' and 'Red Gem' among the best reds. All do well in pots, and both leaves and stems are less prone to droop than most, which is important for exhibitors.

Tulipa subgenus Eriostemones:
T. cretica

A short-stemmed, wine-glass type tulip with pink-tinged white flowers and purpled-edged narrow, sharply 'V'-shaped, twisted, prostrate leaves. This lovely April-flowering species seems to like pots and does well from seed. It is one of the four/five species[3] from Crete. In my garden it shows shoots in November.

T. orthopoda (*T. bifloriformis*)

The white flowers with a yellow centre, close to those of *T. bifloriformis*, have very short stems. For me, it is the first to bloom, arriving in late February or early March.

T. orphanidea (Whittallii Group) AGM

This attractive, wine-glass type tulip, up to 45cm (18in), has slim yellow flowers streaked orange to green. Flourishing in pots, it is a splendid species with unusual colour shades.

T. sprengeri

Until recently, *T. sprengeri* (pictured) was thought to be extinct in its Turkish habitat. The goblet-profiled, brilliant red flowers with bronze to yellow centres appear in late May and into June. It sets prolific amounts of seed, which propagates readily, flowering in four years and pops up in all areas of the garden. Despite also reaching 45cm (18in), it stands up well to bad weather. There is no need to try it in pots, I just enjoy it in the open garden.

Red-flowered cultivars of *T. linifolia* – a species well suited to pot cultivation (*photo* **John Page**)

T. tarda AGM (*T. urumiensis* AGM)

Short, no higher than 10cm (4in), this starry tulip has yellow tepals with white tips. It produces two or three flowers per stem. Very hardy, it flowers in April. It grows anywhere and naturalises quickly, so much so that it can become a weed (but a nice weed!). Grown under glass and in pots, it becomes very lax and lanky. *T. urumiensis* is very similar to *T. tarda*, but with a larger area of yellow inside the tepals and hardly any white. It flowers early to mid-April. It can be good in pots but flowers better in the open garden.

T. turkestanica AGM

This tulip has many small, white, starry flowers with yellow-centred tepals and up to five blooms per stem. Flowering in late March to early April, it is excellent in pots. There is said to be a commercial variety that is taller, with black anthers. I seem to have both forms.

T. biflora

This species is difficult to separate from *T. turkestanica* and one of the two forms of *T. turkestanica* above may in fact be *T. biflora*.

T. polychroma, a synonym of *T. biflora*, has distinctively globe-shaped white flowers. The numerous blooms per stem open well with a bit of warmth and sun. It grows well in pots.

T. neustruevae (*T. dasystemon*)
This has two or three starry yellow flowers to each stem. The tepals are sometimes white-tipped with a bronze outer shading.

Tulipa subgenus Orithyia:
T. heterophylla
This low-stemmed species has small, nodding, yellow flowers, striped grey or black outside. For me it seems to be reluctant to open fully, even in good sunlight. Leaves are dark green.

Tulipa subgenus Tulipa:
T. greigii
The large, wine-glass type flowers of *T. greigii* come in many shades of red, yellow and white, sometimes without the black basal blotch. The leaves are prostrate, broad, curly-edged and sometimes spotted. This species performs well in the garden, but is too big for pots.

A parent of many modern cultivars, its variability in the wild is considerable. The many flower colours sometimes come with streaking or white marbling and veining that may be due to virus. Not all the leaves have the well-known dot-dash patterning. The spectacular flowers of this species can be found in many hill and mountain areas of Eastern Kazakhstan.

T. kolpakowskiana AGM
This medium- to large-sized tulip has starry-type flowers in many colours, mainly yellow, sometimes red, and erect, narrow, grey-green leaves. Some commentators call the red forms *T. ostrowskiana*. It is one of the first to show, new growth appearing as early as November.

T. humilis
Blooming early April, this wine-glass type tulip has short-stemmed purple flowers with a black basal blotch, sometimes edged white. Often available at garden centres, it is easy to grow. There are many named commercial forms, generally regarded as *T. humilis* variants. The lilac form with a yellow centre, which flowers in May, is reliable and good in pots. It is seen in many areas of Eastern Turkey in stony pastures and on rocky hillsides. The 'Eastern Star' form is short, upright and with narrow leaves. It has purple flowers with a yellow centre and seems to be easy. 'Lilliput' has very short-stemmed, dark red flowers although I have failed with this three times.

The wine-glass type *T. humilis* var. *pulchella* (Albocaerulea Oculata Group) has white flowers with a steel-blue centre on short stems. This stunning plant can be difficult in pots but is well worth a try. The name has many versions in commerce.

T. aucheriana AGM (*T. humilis*)
A short-sized tulip, *T. aucheriana* (pictured) has lilac flowers with a yellow centre. Similar to *T. humilis* but usually taller and later-flowering (May). A good performer in pots and reliable, it has been my most successful Show tulip, but needs lots of warmth and light to open fully.

Species tulips only seen in the wild

Tulipa subgenus Tulipa:
T. zenaidae (*T. lehmanniana*)
This short-stemmed tulip has red or yellow flowers and broad, grey-green leaves. It is found in the Merke Gorge in Kazakhstan, in pastureland and on grassy hillsides. I have never found it offered in the trade but have obtained a commercial source for seed.

T. kaufmanniana
Predominantly this has a whitish flower with pink, vertical stripes but in the wild there are many variations. Hotspots are the Dzabagly river valley and pasture and scrub in Siram Su in Eastern Kazakhstan. It has parented many hybrids but I haven't found a commercial source of the true species.

T. julia

Found in many parts of Eastern Turkey and Armenia, this lovely, short-stemmed tulip has red flowers, occasionally yellow and prostrate grey-green leaves. Near Lake Van it grows on dry gravel slopes. It is available commercially.

T. albertii

With red or yellow flowers and broad, grey-green leaves, this occurs in gravel, near-desert conditions in Tamgaly-Tas, Eastern Kazakhstan. I have never found a commercial source.

T. ostrowskiana

This is a small, starry type tulip, also found on gravel slopes in Eastern Kazakhstan. A red form of *T. kolpakowskiana* has been given this name, but flowers seen in Kazakhstan were mostly dingy mauves, browns and oranges.

Tulipa subgenus Eriostemones:

T. doerfleri (T. orphanidea)

A medium-sized tulip with dull-red flowers and a black centre, this fourth Cretan species occurs as a weed of cultivation on the dry, gravelly phrygana (coastal scrub) above Spili.

T. dasystemon

This grows with *T. heterophylla* at the Great Almaty Lake in Eastern Kazakhstan in stony pasture at 2,460m (8070ft), snow lying in the area. Its short-stemmed, yellow flowers can be striped grey to black on the outside. The two species have clearly different bulbs. I have not found a commercial source of the true form.

T. sylvestris

This deep yellow-flowered tulip up to 30cm (12in) has naturalised throughout northern Europe in sites ranging from roadside pastures in the Pindos mountains of Greece to wet meadows in Yorkshire.

Mike Hopkins *has been a member of the Scottish Rock Garden Club since the 1980s. With a special interest in alpine plants, particularly bulbs, he is a renowned exhibitor north of the border.*

The author's most succesful show tulip, *T. aucheriana*, grows well in pots (*photo* **John Page**)

NOTES

[1] See *Daffodil, Snowdrop and Tulip Yearbook* (2019) pp58–60
[2] See note 1, p24
[3] The 'four/five' Cretan tulips are *T. cretica*, *T. saxatilis*, *T. goulimyi*, *T. doerfleri* and *T. bakeri*. The oft-cited seaside location for *T. goulimyi* in the Korikos Peninsula of Crete no longer seems to hold good, as Mike suggests, but there is a credible report of a site for this species higher up among the rocks. Whatever the case, it must be left alone. There are numerous small populations of this species in the Peloponnesian peninsulas, with the same caveat. It is listed in the Greek *Red Data Book* as vulnerable.

New *Tulipa* species published in the past 10 years:
how they are found and described

Sjaak de Groot

***T. berkariensis*, first described in 2019, growing in Aksu Djabagly Reserve, S. Kazakhstan**
(*all photos* **Sjaak de Groot**)

Since the collapse of the Soviet Union and the communist system, travel in Asia has become much easier for both westerners and easterners, leading to an increasing interest in the flora and fauna of countries previously out of bounds. The first travellers were plant and seed collectors, mainly from former Soviet Union countries in the Baltic area and people from the Czech Republic because they spoke a Slavonic language. These were followed by collectors from Western Europe such as Jim and Jenny Archibald and others from several botanic gardens. When the flowers emerged from their collections, several of them turned out to be new to science.

What do we mean by a new species? The obvious answer is that it is one that is new to science, but it is not as easy as it may seem at first glance. Because all species are allied to, or have evolved from other species, you have to compare a potentially new species with all its related taxa. The easiest way to do this is to grow them all under the same conditions because characteristics may vary in different growing circumstances. This necessitates a large collection of the different forms of the species involved. Since they will all share a wide variability in their characteristics, you need to identify those that are the most stable.

In most cases, these will be the tepals, stamens, stigma, ovary, seedpods and seed, the hairiness or otherwise of the plant parts, the shape and colour of the bulb tunic and its inside covering. Where the proper facilities exist, additional non-visible data may be obtained through DNA sequencing of genetic material. The next step is to check these characteristics against the original species description. If then enough differences remain with which the tulip is clearly distinguishable from its relatives, it may safely be described as a new species.

How can you detect a new species in its native habitat? As a rule, you do not come across new species in the wild because they do not normally grow together with other species and you have nothing to compare them with at that particular site. If doubts remain, you take as many detailed photographs as possible of the whole population, plus individual plants and all their chief characteristics, and make a note of anything else that matters so that in the years to come you have the relevant data relating to the plant as it was in nature. Then you have to dig up a plant of the form in the population that is most common so as to examine the key features of the bulb, either to dry it as a herbarium sample, or to collect it for replanting in a collection, all of course with the proper permission and in accordance with local laws.

Another means of detecting potentially undescribed species is to grow plants from seed, either wild collected (this is becoming increasingly difficult due to local laws) or by hand-pollinated seeds from suppliers or seed exchanges, which come with reliable information regarding origin and are sold as *Tulipa* sp. without species names.

A third source is incorrectly-named and undescribed species in the trade, examples of which are *T. kolpakowskiana* and *T. iliensis*. These two have been commercially available since the days of the well-known authority on tulips, Sir A Daniel Hall[1], yet both belong in fact to a hitherto undescribed species of the *T. ferganica* alliance. Similar forms grow on the border between Uzbekistan and Tadjikistan, south of the Fergana valley. *T. eichleri* and its named cultivars is another case in point. With its resemblance to *T. fosteriana* and low amount of DNA this species is clearly a tulip from Central Asia and it does not match the *T. eichleri* described by E. Regel from the plant that grows in the Caucasus mountains of Azerbaijan, a tulip with a much higher amount of DNA.

It is important that an entire plant deemed to be a new species is dried with all its characteristics as the holotype. This is deposited in an official herbarium – one normally associated with a university – and the name of this herbarium and the plant's accession number must be mentioned in the material section of the description.

Tulip species described in the past ten years

2010
• *Tulipa koyuncui* Described by I Eker & M Babaç in the *Nordic Journal of Botany* 28(3): 325 (324–328; figs.1–2, map) (2010) as a small yellow Biflora tulip from the higher altitudes around 2,000m (6,500ft) of the Van province of SE Turkey. It is described as a yellow-flowering tulip only but I have seen photos of a population where the yellows were mixed with white forms.
• *Tulipa albanica* Described by Kit Tan & L Shuka in *Phytotaxa* 10: 19 (17–24); figs.2–4) (2010) as a new tulip species from serpentine soil in NE Albania. This new species belongs to the Gesneriana tulips growing in the Balkan Peninsular, the steppes of E. Europe, the Caucasus and the Central Asian steppes. Tulips in this group are the ancestors of today's long-stemmed garden forms recognisable by their slender habit and wide, protruding stigmas. *T. albanica* grows in yellow and red flowering forms in mixed populations.

2011
• *Tulipa talassica* Described by G Lazkov in *Turczaninowia* (14)3: 11 (2011) after a tulip species in the Kolpakowskianae section that grows wild on the south-facing, stony slopes of the western Kyrgyz Alatau bordering on the Talas river valley in NW Kyrgyzstan. This species occurs mainly as a small, yellow tulip with some red forms. It grows on chalk, in contrast to other members of the Kolpakowskianae section, which occur mainly in slightly acidic soils.

2012
• *Tulipa lemmersii* Described by B J M Zonneveld, A Peterse and J de Groot in *Plant Systematics and Evolution* 298(1): 87–92 (2012) as a short-stemmed, early-flowering yellow Kolpakowskiana from the stony rim of the Mashad Canyon in S.Kazakhstan. It is named after W Lemmers[2], a retired bulb grower and passionate traveller to sites in the wild where tulips grow naturally.
• *Tulipa kolbintsevii* (pictured) Described by

B J M Zonneveld in *Plant Systematics and Evolution* 298, 1293–1296 (2012) as a new tulip in the Eriostemones subgenus from the northern valleys of the Dzungarian Alatau in East Kazakhstan. Commonly flowering as a single bloom, this small white tulip has the lowest amount of DNA in the whole subgenus.
• *Tulipa kosovarica* Described by Kit Tan, L Shuka & Krasniqi in *Phytotaxa* 62: 2–3 (2012) from serpentine soil in SW Kosovo. This mainly red-flowering species (some whites occur as well) also belongs to the Gesnerianae species like *T. albanica*.

2013
• *Tulipa ivasczenkoae* Described by Epiktetov & Belyalov in *Turczaninowia* 16(3): 5 (2013) as a tulip in the Lanatae section. It is stoloniferous, smaller and later-flowering, but otherwise similar in habit to *T. fosteriana*. Named after the Kazakhstan botanist Dr Anna Ivaschenko, it grows in East Kazakhstan in the Sholac Mountains, the most western part of the Dzungarian Alatau.

T. kolbintsevii, described in 2012, in cultivation (above left); *T. intermedia*, described in 2014, in the Fergana valley, E Uzbekistan (above right); *T. jacquesii*, described in 2015, in cultivation (above far right)

2014

• ***Tulipa auliekolica*** Described by Perezhogin in *Novosti Sistematiki Vysshikh Rastenii* 45: 145 (2014) after tulips found in the Aulicola district of the Kostanay province, Kazakhstan. The description indicates a small yellow-flowering Biflora tulip. In the same article Perezhogin also describes *T. turgaica*, a species found in the Zhangeldin district of the Kostanay province. The description indicates a yellow-flowering tulip with some similarity to *T. biebersteiniana*.

• *Tulipa narcissicum* Described by N Y Stepanova in *Botanicheskii Zhurnal* (Moscow and Leningrad) 99(10): 1121 (2014). This is a new species in the *T. biebersteiniana* alliance. Mainly a triploid species, it is larger and of a paler yellow colour than *T. biebersteiniana*, growing as a steppe tulip in Russia, NW of the Caspian Sea.

• *Tulipa akamasica* Described by Christodolou, Hand & Charalamb in *Flora Mediterranea* 24: 208 (2014) from a tulip in a single location on the Akamas Peninsula of Cyprus. It is a red-flowering relative of *T. hageri*.

• *Tulipa intermedia* (pictured) Described by K Tojibaev & J de Groot in *Nordic Journal of Botany* 32(5): 546 (2014). It is found in the Fergana Valley of Uzbekistan. A small, pale yellow form in the species group around *T. korolkowii*. The tulip described in the same article as *Tulipa intermedia* var. *korolkowioides* K Tojibaev & J de Groot in *Nordic Journal of Botany* 32(5): 546 (2014) is a bright red flowering form.

2015

• *Tulipa luanica* Described by F Milaku in *Annales Botanici Fennici* 52 (5–6): 316 (2015). A pink-flowering Gesneriad tulip growing wild in SW Kosovo on limestone slopes, partly in the same area as *T. kosovarica*.

• *Tulipa jacquesii* (pictured) Described by B J M Zonneveld in *Phytotaxa* 218(2): 185 (2015) and named after the author of this article. It is a small, early-flowering, white tulip in the

Eriostemones subgenus, growing wild on white kaolin soil in W. Kyrgyzstan. *T. jacquesii* is recognisable by its thick leaf structure, somewhat similar to that of *T. regelii*.

2016
• *Tulipa cinnabarina* subsp. *toprakii* Described by H Yıldırım & I Eker in *Phytokeys* 69: 66 (2016). This is a small, red, single-flowered Eriostemone tulip belonging to the Saxatilis section. It grows wild in SW Turkey. Together with *T. cinnabarina*, it belongs to a group of tulips in evolutionary terms between the species around *T. hageri* and *T. humilis*.

2017
• *Tulipa zonneveldii* Described by J de Groot and K Tojibaev in *International Rock Gardener* 93: 20 (2017), this is a small single or multi-flowered yellow tulip, which, in evolutionary terms, is intermediate between the species group around *T. ferganica* and tulips of the Vinistriata/Spiranthera section. It grows in the Chatcal mountains of W. Kyrgyzstan.

2019
• ***Tulipa berkariensis*** (pictured) Described by J Rukšāns in *International Rock Gardener* 109: [33], photographs (2019) this is a variably-coloured species in the Vinistriata/Spiranthera section, growing in S.Kazakhstan. It differs from the related *T. kaufmanniana* by its mainly two leaves, stoloniferous habit, lower DNA amount and more northerly occurrence.

2020
• *Tulipa dianaeverettiae* Described by J de Groot & B J M Zonneveld in *International Rock Gardener* 122: 7, photographs (2020). This white Eriostemones tulip grows in the Altai mountains of Kazakhstan to Mongolia. It is distinguishable from other members of the Biflora group, being the only species with a small dome on the top of the seedpods.
• *Tulipa annae* (pictured) Described by J de Groot and B J M Zonneveld in the same *International Rock Gardener* article as the

T. annae, described in 2020, on the Marble Pass, E Kazakhstan

above, this species is in the *T. altaica* alliance in the Kolpakowskianae section. It is smaller than *T. altaica*, with yellow flowers and leaves in the form of a rosette at soil level.

NOTES

[1] Sir A Daniel Hall Chief Scientific Adviser, Ministry of Agriculture, 1920–27, Director, John Innes Horticultural Institution, 1927–1939, author of the first major tulip monograph *The Genus Tulipa* (1940).
[2] Wim Lemmers, who sadly recently passed away, was a member of the former RHS Daffodil and Tulip Committee and had also been involved in Daffodil and Tulip Trials at RHS Garden Wisley. An obituary will be included in the 2021 Yearbook.

Sjaak de Groot *gained experience of bulbs in the nursery trade and built up an extensive collection. His travels to see tulips in their native habitat in Central Asia led to his ten-year term as Chairman of the Special Bulb Committee of the Dutch KAVB*

Looking back

Teresa Clements

In an attempt to catch the eye of the public at the RHS Tulip Competition at Harlow Carr Gardens 2020, a display about exhibitors' favourite tulips seemed like a good idea. Alas, the competition was cancelled but here is a preview for a display in 2021[1]. Looking back at past copies of the Daffodil and Tulip Yearbook provided a rich source of material, these excerpts speak for themselves.

1946 My Favourite Tulips by E A Bowles
p141 T. 'Zomerschoon'
'Zomerschoon ' still heads my list as first favourite. I find that I wrote of it in 1913. "It is seen at its best in the morning sunlight, and when the first blossoms open I find it hard to tear myself away from them, so intensely do I enjoy the glow of the blend of salmon and primrose tints in their cups."

T. '**Zomerschoon**' (*all photos* **Teresa Clements**)

p144 *T. sprengeri*
A man blind from birth said he thought the colour red must be like the sound of a trumpet – I think of that when *T. sprengeri*, the latest to flower, opens its yellow backed petals to display the startling scarlet of their inner surface. Even *Habranthus pratensis*, which flowers about the same time, has not so strong and clear a tone to represent in colour the clarion note of a trumpet. Is it too fanciful to call *T. sprengeri* the bugler that sounds the Last Post for the close of another year's Tulip season?

1954 Holland in Tulip Time
by Guy L. Wilson VMH
pp137–8 T. 'Prinses Irene'
One of the beds out in the open lawn, contained a wonderful dwarf variety named 'Prinses Irene', which is said to be a sport from 'Couleur Cardinal'. I thought this one of the most outstanding varieties that I saw: it was of sturdy dwarf habit having deep blue-green foliage which carried a greyish bloom, and stiff deep purple-bronze stems while the colouring of the flowers was a wonderfully beautiful rich soft Dutch orange or deep bricky orange, brighter at the edge of the petals which bore an exterior flame of soft dusky smoky purple which blended into the ground colour: the interior of the flower was a glowing old golden orange. The whole plant made an extraordinarily rich and beautiful colour effect.

1960 Raising and Introducing New Tulips by D W Lefeber
p21 *T.* 'Oxford'

Out of the last mentioned crossing I obtained the nowadays well known Darwin hybrid tulips, among which my favourite ones: 'London': one of the largest; earliest flowering; suited for forcing.

Vermilion flushed scarlet, base black, edged yellow. 'Roosevelt': one of the best Darwin shapes; extra strong and large flowers. Brilliant orange scarlet, base black, yellow margined. 'Oxford': most elegant and perfect shaped. One of the brightest colours, orange, red flushed, yellow base.

The yearbooks make fascinating reading, they are full of information, advice and comments on the concerns of their particular eras, many of which are still relevant. The writing is fresh and enthusiastic and the writers voice their personal opinions in an engaging and entertaining way. The light-hearted accounts by Guy Wilson of his trips to America and the Netherlands were full of amusing incidents and details that were a delight to read.

The three examples in this article were chosen because we can now illustrate the chosen tulips with recent colour images. Other cultivars were mentioned that, unfortunately, no longer exist – but don't let that put you off a stroll through the pages with some of the great names from the past. A set of copies of the Daffodil and Tulip Yearbooks can be found in the Lindley Library.

Teresa Clements *was Secretary of the Wakefield and North of England Tulip Society for ten years and is now Chair of the RHS Bulb Committee*

NOTES

[1] The RHS Flower Show at Harlow Carr will be held in the summer of 2021, subject to Covid restrictions. For details of RHS shows planned for 2021, please see p123.

T. **'Prinses Irene'**

T. 'Oxford'

Springfields Gardens Festival of Tulips 2020

David Norton and Andy Boyton

Springfields Gardens in Lincolnshire opened in 1966 as a shop window for the British flower bulb industry (*photo* **Springfields Gardens**)

When Head Gardener Andy Boynton and his fellow gardeners started planting more than 100,000 spring bulbs back in October/November 2019 for Lincolnshire's Springfields Gardens Festival of Tulips 2020, we could not have foreseen that by the time the tulips came into flower there would be no visitors to enjoy the displays we had created.

Sadly, the Covid-19 coronavirus lockdown meant that everyone was at home and not able to travel to any of the country's public gardens to admire the traditional colourful welcome of spring bulbs coming into bloom.

Since it first opened in 1966 as a shop

window for the British flower bulb industry, this has been the first occasion when Springfields Gardens could not open its gates to enable the public to enjoy the spring daffodils and tulips. Although tulips are no longer grown in the surrounding fields on the outskirts of the market town of Spalding, the displays featured in the gardens have been a continuous reminder of the part that tulips have played in the horticultural heritage of the area.

For more than 50 years these flowers have celebrated the colourful landscape of the fields around us, when they toured the town as part of the world-famous Spalding Tulip Parade in specially constructed floats decorated with thousands of tulip heads cut off to help grow the bulbs for lifting and selling. The celebration of tulips in this manner attracted the attention of the World Tulip Society, which Spalding joined as the UK's representative. We followed this by hosting a World Tulip Summit in 2008 in the town as part of the celebrations for the Fiftieth Spalding Flower Parade.

2020 composition

But now in 2020 much has changed, not only because of Covid 19. Tulips are no longer grown in the area (though they are on a limited scale in Norfolk) and the unique celebration event that was the Spalding Flower Parade came to an end in 2013. So, what would tulip enthusiasts and visiting families have been able to see at this year's Festival of Tulips? Our Head Gardener, Andy Boyton, now explains what we had in mind for this year's composition:

"Our garden team arranged displays in various formats throughout the 6 hectares (15 acres) of show gardens, which included woodland walks, landscaped beds, designer gardens by celebrities such as Chris Beardshaw and Kim Wilde and water features. The planting schemes were based on three styles to display the 300 plus different tulip cultivars for maximum effect.

Firstly, we mix-planted with seasonal bedding or under-planted in the perennial beds with either a combination of viola, or polyanthus or wallflower. A particularly good cultivar we use is *Erysimum* 'Aida', one of our favourites because it produces scented flowers blooming all through the winter into late spring. We also used hyacinths, daffodils and other species bulbs to give a longer display time, hopefully from March to early May.

Secondly, we planted the more expensive and newer tulip cultivars in clumps. We felt that this would showcase the beauty of the flowers and their fabulous range of colours in a better way and would also provide good photographic opportunities. Sadly, as things turned out, this was not to be. However, any cultivars that we use do lend themselves to this method of display.

An old cultivar, also very popular with our visitors, is *Tulipa* 'Dom Pedro', a Single Late Breeder Tulip first introduced before 1911. With its 70cm (28in) stem bearing a Morocco red flower with an olive-streaked yellow base – a delight to see with its almost metallic tepals – this is normally only found in historical collections.

Moving on to the newer end of tulip cultivars that we have on show is the aptly-named Double Late *T*. 'Ice Cream', a cone of pure white surrounded by strawberry-pink tepals. It is an example of some of the modern introductions, as is the very strange Double Late *T*. 'Exquisit', which resembles an artichoke before the deep purple peony flowers fully open.

Thirdly, we planted in mass drifts of colours, with a minimum of 500 bulbs per cultivar, 50,000 bulbs in all, echoing the tradition of tulip displays that would have been seen here back in the 1970s.

A new introduction that we wanted to roll out this year was the use of NFC (Near-Field Communication) on our plant and information boards enabling visitors to use a smart phone to scan a label (which has a data tag embedded) and allowing them to read key

Tulipa 'Banya Luka' (Darwin Hybrid Group) encircles a tree trunk, with an outer ring of yellow *Tulipa* 'Hamilton' (Fringed Group) (*photo* **John Page**)

information about a particular cultivar of bulbs displayed on their phone. As it turned out, the only way to experience these wonderful displays was via a YouTube video linked to the Springfields website – www.springfieldsfestivalgardens.org.uk!"

David Norton adds "while the video picture album does give a visual impression of what this year's Tulip Festival sought to offer, it in no way replaces the genuine pleasure of seeing real live tulips in their full colours in their various settings in the garden, with the background of trees, the sound of birds, the water features and the atmosphere created by the tens of thousands of visitors who come to enjoy our Festival.

"We will soon be planting bulbs for our 2021 Show and hopefully, when the tulips are in bloom next spring, people will once again be able to share again with us the joyous feelings that tulips give and discover that the Festival offers so much more to visitors than these wonderful bulbs".

David Norton *is Chief Executive of the charity Springfields Horticultural Society, which manages the Springfields Festival Gardens as a free-to-enter, all-year-round public attraction*

Andy Boyton *is Head Gardener at Springfields Gardens, whose many activities include overall supervision of the planning of the annual spring Festival whereby tradition tulips have such a prominent position*

Popular tulip cultivars for exhibition

Teresa and Jason Clements

Which tulip cultivars perform consistently well on the showbench? Exhibitors are always looking for tulips that meet the judging standards but it is surprising how often enthusiastic exhibitors overlook the basic rule for single tulips – to have six tepals and six stamens, the characteristic feature of the *Liliaceae* family. They carefully select and stage their blooms only to realise too late that the vase of three has been rendered Not According to Schedule (NAS) because one flower has extra flower parts, as can arise with cultivars.

The condition of the flower is also important – does it look healthy and fresh? Any signs of disease, such as a disruption of the colour due to Tulip Breaking Virus (TBV), or brown marks due to hail damage or fungal disease, spoil both the appearance of a bloom and its chances of winning. Exhibitors should aim to show tulips that are uniform in size, colour and condition; the tepals should be clean and without debris, such as pollen, dust and insects; and blooms should be carefully staged and presented to look their best.

With the above considerations in mind it is interesting to see which tulips have performed consistently well over the past 30 years. The data in the table represents the top 25 winners since 1990 from Tulip Competitions held by:
• The Wakefield and North of England Tulip Society
• The Northern Horticultural Society at the Harrogate Spring Flower Show
• The Royal Horticultural Society's Tulip Competition held alongside the Late Daffodil Competition.

There are some gaps in the data that we

Single late tulip 'Maureen' tops the list of winning cultivars (*all photos* **T Clements**)

have been unable to fill due to the Coronavirus pandemic and current lockdown restrictions. Even so, a total of 162 names appear on the list, of which we are focusing on the top 25.

Looking back at prize-winning tulip cultivars brought to mind some familiar old names. Topping the list is *T.* 'Maureen' with 42 wins over 31 years from 1989 to 2019. In second place, *T.* 'Menton' has almost as long a period of success and won on 26 occasions. *T.* 'World's Favourite' and *T.* 'Toyota', third and fourth in the rankings, are still being shown but *T.* 'Vivex', in fifth place, had a brief period of success from 1996 to 2009 yet these days is seldom seen at competitions.

Top 25 winners from the past 30 years of tulip competitions

Position	Cultivar	No. of wins	Earliest year	Latest year	Span
1	'Maureen'	42	1989	2019	31
2	'Menton'	26	1992	2019	28
3	'World's Favourite'	15	2002	2019	18
4	'Toyota'	13	2006	2018	13
5	'Vivex'	11	1996	2009	14
6	'Big Smile'	10	2002	2013	12
7	'Golden Parade'	9	1992	2016	25
8	'Orange Princess'	8	2003	2018	16
8	'World Peace'	8	2009	2019	11
10	'Dordogne'	7	2005	2018	14
10	'Spring Green'	7	1992	2019	28
12	'Hilary Clinton'	6	2001	2006	6
13	'Ad Rem'	5	2007	2017	11
13	'Ballade'	5	1992	2018	27
13	'Bright Parrot'	5	2012	2016	5
13	'Olympic Flame'	5	1996	2014	19
13	'Pink Impression'	5	1999	2016	18
13	'Purissima'	5	1996	2010	15
19	'Angelique'	4	1994	2017	24
19	'Angel's Wish'	4	2012	2016	5
19	'Burgundy Lace'	4	1989	2004	16
19	'Flaming Parrot'	4	1997	2019	23
19	'Golden Oxford'	4	1997	2005	9
19	'Mrs. John T. Scheepers'	4	1994	2011	18
19	'Pieter d'Leur'	4	2002	2010	9

Tulipa 'Maureen'

Way ahead of other cultivars is *T*. 'Maureen' (pictured), a single late tulip. Registered in 1950 and described as 'marble white', this old favourite performs reliably well. *T*. 'Maureen' seems far less predisposed to producing extra petals and stamens than other cultivars.

The flowers are an elongated egg shape and are held upright on long, sturdy stems. The tepals have a stiff, waxy texture and are held tightly together as the flower matures. This maintains the smooth, elegant shape of the flower, which also has a long lifespan.

Outdoors in strong sunlight or in a warm room the flowers open to reveal the base of the tepals and the six filaments, which are pale apricot in colour. The slim anthers bear yellow pollen and extend a little beyond the small, neat, cream-coloured stigma. The open flowers release an unpleasant scent, an unusual attribute for a tulip that is unlikely to be noticed in the garden, but in a warm, confined space, such as in a car on the way to a competition, it soon becomes evident.

Away from the demands of competitions, *T*. 'Maureen' is a useful, reliable bedding tulip.

Deep pink and white *Tulipa* 'Toyota' performs well on the show bench and in pots or the open garden

At about 70cm (28in) tall, its robust, long-lasting flowers on strong stems are held well above the foliage to give a good uniform display. They are comparatively resistant to poor weather conditions and, because they are white, show no detrimental effect if infected with TBV, which affects the synthesis and distribution of anthocyanins in the tepals of most tulips with coloured flowers.

For exhibitors and gardeners alike, reliable *T.* 'Maureen', with its cool, elegant appeal, is a worthy candidate to top the list and it received an AGM from the RHS in 1993.

Tulipa 'Menton'

With 26 recorded wins, *T.* 'Menton', in second place, is also a single late tulip. Registered in 1971, with a lengthy description of its colour, it is a sport of pink *T.* 'Renown', an old favourite of exhibitors in the 1960s and 1970s.

The exterior of the tepals of *T.* 'Menton' is china rose with edges lightly feathered with orange; the interior is "poppy red with a white vein, base naples yellow and white, blotched greenish, anthers yellow" – a complicated description of an attractive flower.

T. 'Menton' has a soft gradation of colour that enhances the shape of the flower, giving it more appeal than its plain pink predecessor, *T.* 'Renown', which one grower regarded as 'pink blobs' – not the most complimentary description! *T.* 'Menton' became a popular tulip for competitions and success has established it as an exhibitor's favourite so it is now seen far more often than *T.* 'Renown'.

T. 'Menton' also performs well as a garden plant with tough 65cm (26in) stems supporting its large, egg-shaped flowers and the tepals have a fine, waxy bloom that gives them some protection in poor weather.

It received an RHS AGM in 2008.
(In 10th place on the list, *T.* 'Dordogne',
registered in 1991, is a sport of *T.* 'Menton'.)

Tulipa 'World's Favourite', 'Toyota' and 'Vivex'

In positions 3 and 4, *T.* 'World's Favourite', a
Darwin hybrid, and *T.* 'Toyota', another single
late tulip, have similar scores and a similar
period of success. Number 5 on the list is the
Darwin hybrid *T.* 'Vivex', not far behind them
for its tally of first prizes but, although
popular from 1996 to 2009, it has now
disappeared from competitions, possibly due
to a lack of availability. *T.* 'World's Favourite'
has been successful since 2002. Similar in
colour to *T.* 'Vivex', both having tepals that
are red with a yellow margin, they were in
direct competition from 2002 until the decline
of *T.* 'Vivex' after 2009 left *T.* 'World's
Favourite' as the dominant Darwin hybrid.

Tulipa 'World's Favourite' was registered
in 1992 and the registration details include
ten lines of description regarding its colour,
including reds – tomato, capsicum, blood;
yellows – aureolin and lemon; and willow
green. In common with most Darwin hybrids
it is very robust. It grows to a height of 45cm
(18in) and is an excellent garden plant. It is
popular for its good performance and flowers
earlier in the season than the single late tulips,
so is particularly useful for early competitions.
It received an RHS AGM in 2010.

Tulipa 'Toyota' (pictured) was registered in
1984 and is a single late tulip. The tepals are
deep pink with a white margin and the base is
yellow edged with violet; the anthers are dark
grey. The flowers are an elongated egg shape
and the tepals are pointed rather than
rounded at the top. The flower opens more
widely than those above, which gives them a
crown-like upper profile. A vigorous grower, it
performs well in pots or in the open garden.
The large flowers on flexible 65cm (26in)
stems may make them unsuitable for a very
windy location but they have appealing,
graceful movement among other plants.

Tulipa 'Vivex' (pictured) was registered in
1960. Although once very popular, it is now
difficult to obtain in the UK.

Choice cultivars

The tulips further down the list are too
numerous to mention individually, which
demonstrates how many cultivars there are to
choose from when buying bulbs for exhibition
or the garden. The cut-flower industry also
has a huge influence on which bulbs are
propagated and made available for retail. The
work of the RHS Bulb Committee, the AGM,
horticultural competitions, shows and trials,
together with reports in publications such as
this, all provide information and advice that
helps in selecting bulbs that will perform best
in the appropriate setting.

Jason Clements *has been Treasurer of the
Wakefield and North of England Tulip Society
for twelve years and maintains the Society's
database and Show software*

**Despite its early success, *T.* 'Vivex'
is now difficult to obtain**

People and awards

JAN PENNINGS RETIRES AS RHS BULB COMMITTEE CHAIRMAN

At the end of 2019, Jan Pennings stepped down as Chairman of the Royal Horticultural Society (RHS) Bulb Committee. He had been Chairman for six years and chaired his last meeting on 14 November 2019.

Jan had a great impact on the Bulb Committee, he took on the role of Chairman a year after the committee's remit and title had changed from the Daffodil and Tulip Committee to the Bulb Committee. With careful judgement and great purpose, he held the committee together and took it forward and was always fair in his treatment of all the members. This was accomplished with English as his second language to his native Dutch.

Jan never wavered in his drive to promote the committee, its members and the bulbs that bring us all together. He had the foresight and determination to take us for meetings in the Netherlands and Belfast in addition to involving us in shows, meetings and other events all over the United Kingdom. He was a real trailblazer and we all benefited from his energy, ambition and enthusiasm.

Bulb Committee members have learned about the wider, commercial side of bulb cultivation as well as sharing their specialist interests with Jan. Many will have broadened the range of bulbs in their gardens by growing samples that he generously provided. He and his wife Ans have also been kind and welcoming hosts to many visitors during Jan's time as Chairman. I can think of two occasions on which they have welcomed a coachload of visitors to their home, where there was always a warm welcome, something to eat and drink and a big smile. Our thanks are due to Jan and Ans for their remarkable hospitality over many years.

Teresa Clements and Jan Pennings 14 November 2019 at the last RHS Bulb Committee meeting chaired by Jan (*photo* **Michael Pitcher/RHS**)

Although Jan has retired as Chairman, he remains an active member of the Bulb Committee. He retains a passionate interest in bulbs and will always be an ambassador for the RHS and bulbs in particular. His time at the helm of the Bulb Committee meant a great deal to him and he made a touching and memorable farewell to us as Chairman.

In tribute to his service to the RHS, he was presented with a splendid book and a Tulip tree, *Liriodendron tulipifera*, together with gifts from his many friends. The bulbs he gave us will be a lasting reminder of his friendship.

For me, as his successor, Jan will be a very hard act to follow but I am happy to say we can all look forward to seeing him at future meetings and, together with Ans, at many events to come.

Teresa Clements

RHS VEITCH MEMORIAL MEDAL AWARDED TO IAN YOUNG

I was very pleased to be asked to provide a tribute to Ian Young on his award of the Veitch Memorial Medal, as he has long been a bulb 'hero' of mine. His very well known 'Bulb Log' on the Scottish Rock Garden Club's website has been written every week for more than 17 years and is a fantastic source of information for all things bulbous.

The Veitch Memorial Medal honours individuals for their 'exceptional involvement in the advancement of the science, art and practice of horticulture'. Any long-standing devotee of the Bulb Log will know that Ian doesn't take received wisdom as truth, unless he has experimented and proved it to his own satisfaction. Many of the methods I use in my own garden have been driven by that research, which is superbly illustrated by detailed photographs. His contribution to the science and practice of bulb culture is valued by all his readers. The 'art' part is covered by his other skills as an artist and sculptor of note.

Ian also served the RHS Joint Rock Garden Plant Committee between 2001 and 2018.

Along with his wife Maggi (Margaret), he has been a mainstay of the Scottish Rock Garden Club for many years, including serving as President and Show Secretary, and is often to be seen calmly and competently dealing with the technical side of things at events.

His seemingly boundless energy and enthusiasm belies the fact that he has long-term health problems, yet he has travelled the

Ian Young in his garden (*photo* **Margaret Young**)

globe speaking at prestigious conferences, appeared on television, written numerous articles, and been part of BBC Radio Scotland's Beechgrove phone-in panel, also consulting on horticultural matters for radio programmes.

In 2007 Ian and Maggi were awarded the Queen Elizabeth the Queen Mother Medal by the Royal Caledonian Horticultural Society for their outstanding contribution to horticulture, and had the honour of having a crocus named for them both by Jānis Rukšāns – *Crocus youngiorum*.

Ian is a great ambassador for the culture of all things alpine and bulbous, taking his message all over the world, both in person and virtually via the Bulb Log, and is an exceptionally worthy recipient of the award.

Anne Wright

Two unregistered daffodils selected by Ian Young 'Craigton Clumper' 10Y-Y (left) and 'Craigton Chorister' 10W-W (right) (*photo* **Anne Wright**)

PETER BARR MEMORIAL CUP 2020 AWARDED TO CHRISTINE SKELMERSDALE

Alan Street

Christine Skelmersdale (*photo* **Christine Skelmersdale)**

Out of the 111 recipients of the Peter Barr Memorial Cup, awarded annually for good work in connection with daffodils (twice awarded jointly), only 12 have been women, so it seems fitting that Christine holds the torch in her turn, not least because she, like Peter Barr VMH, has spent her whole working life involved with all things daffodillian!

Born in Southampton but spending her formative years in the Yorkshire Dales where both parents were passionate gardeners and good friends with Geoffrey Smith, Curator of nearby Harlow Carr, little did she know how infectious horticulture could be, but the seeds, so to speak, had been unwittingly sown.

After studying geography and education at the University of Nottingham, she went to Zambia to teach, where she met Roger, a trained horticulturist whom she later married. In 1972 they set up Broadleigh Gardens near Taunton, Somerset, based on the Alec Gray collection of daffodils. Alec was also a recipient of the Cup in 1945. They moved hundreds of thousands of bulbs to their new site at, appropriately, Barr House. Soon after Roger took up work in the House of Lords leaving Christine to run the fledgling nursery along with bringing up two young children. No time to be idle then or since.

Her boundless energy and enthusiasm has shown itself in the many horticultural committees on which she has worked over several decades. Christine joined the then RHS Daffodil and Tulip Committee in the mid 1980s, was a member of the RHS Council for 11 years, a flower show judge for over 30 years, Garden Godparent for RHS Rosemoor for 12 years and a former Vice Chairman of the RHS Bulb Committee. As President of the Association of Friends of the University of Bristol Botanic Garden, she was a member of the Steering Committee responsible for moving and making the new Garden. Her well

deserved VMH was awarded in 2009.

Two books, *Bulbs* (WI creative gardening series) and her *Gardener's Guide to Bulbs* contain many authoritative references to daffodils and she continues to write extensively for many publications including this Yearbook, sharing her acute observations of growing, showing and knowing her trade. At the 2004 World Daffodil Convention at Vincent Square in London, she put on a huge display of Alec Gray's work and breeding that was much admired and testament to her work at keeping much of his legacy alive.

When asked to name her finest daffodil show Christine had no hesitation in remembering her display at a Harrogate Spring Show in the late 1970s for which she was awarded a Large Gold Medal.

I have many memories of Christine's 40 years of displays of daffodils and other bulbs at the Chelsea Flower Show and spring shows at Vincent Square. The outstanding memory is of the large numbers of daffodils shown growing in pots, in perfect condition and full of flower towards the end of May every year – one of the most difficult skills to get right. However this was all well within her stride and just another of the many she has mastered over a lifetime spent with flowers.

Christine's promotion of small daffodils in catalogues, displays at shows and superb talks to gatherings both small and large has done much to cement their place as popular plants with enthusiastic gardeners. She is a most worthy recipient of this prestigious award.

(photo): Camilla Bassett-Smith

Obituaries

Colin Mason (*photo* **Hugh Mason**)

G. 'Kathleen Ferrier' (*photo* **Matt Bishop**)

COLIN MASON

Before snowdrops became the horticultural phenomenon they are today, there was a decidedly lean period where almost all new snowdrop cultivars originated with a comparatively tiny cast of characters up until the mid-1990s. Colin Mason (1927–2019) became a central figure in this group.

His introduction came about through a chance meeting with Richard Nutt, whose name was familiar through his periodic articles on snowdrops, at a dinner with fellow engineers. This, in turn led to invitations to snowdrop lunches given by Richard at Great Barfield, Bradenham and Primrose Warburg at South Hayes, Oxford where plants and information on snowdrops was then just about the only place to acquire the newest cultivars.

Colin, along with Ronald Mackenzie, who established the Snowdrop Company, was another early pioneer in the application of twin-scaling as a means of propagation to snowdrops and this revolutionised the speed at which new and old, rare cultivars could be brought to market, while making more certain the future of new selections where the stocks might be limited to just a few bulbs.

Colin was modest, mild-mannered, with a happy-go-lucky approach to life that endeared him to a large circle of friends with whom he maintained a voluminous correspondence that he kept neatly filed. He was a meticulous keeper of records and habitually carried a Dictaphone (or 'squalk-box', as he used to call it) and especially at Galanthophile gatherings he would record snippets of information about newly named snowdrops and their origins that would be religiously transcribed for later reference. As such and during the preparation of the text for *Snowdrops: A Monograph of Cultivated Galanthus* (2001), Colin was a valuable source of contemporaneous information.

By the late 1990s, Colin was caring for Bridget, his wife of 36 years, who suffered from muscular dystrophy and died in 1998. By this time the garden at Fieldgate Lane Kenilworth was home to one of the country's most substantial snowdrop collections and was increasingly a Mecca for those wishing to see the latest introductions. The assemblage of snowdrops were supplemented with a collection of *Iris unguicularis*, the odd crocus and niche daffodil although he laughingly would tolerate prevalent jibes at the 'Mason's monoculture'!

As to Colin's own tastes, his preference was for the species of *Galanthus* and he travelled extensively to see them in their wild state and indeed his first introduction 'Yamanlar' was from wild material brought in 1972 from the mountain of that name close to Izmir in Turkey.

Although he could be quite verbal in his distain at the idea of deliberately created hybrids, Colin was not beyond gently nudging the process by collecting and sowing seed of cultivars where he saw potential for their features being passed on and enhanced. In this way the garden became the source of some fine seedlings. These would usually be given the appellation to denote their origin, starting with the late, large-flowered 'Fieldgate Superb' (1996) and its rounded-flowered possible sibling 'Fieldgate Fugue' (1998). 'Fieldgate Prelude' (selected 1998) was isolated from *G. elwesii* 'Mrs Macnamara' for its diffuse inner marking in 1998 and in the following year 'Fieldgate Forte' from seedlings of *G. × valentinei* 'Modern Art' and 'Fieldgate Tiffany', for its large, puckered outer segments in 2001.

More recently, Colin noticed a very fine seedling with generously green-tipped outer segments that he named *G. elwesii* 'Kathleen Ferrier' after the famous contralto whose singing he greatly admired. He also selected from a patch of the inverse-poculiform 'Trymlet' seedlings, the strikingly double-marked *G. plicatus* 'Fieldgate Sophie' named for his daughter. Through his sales and through his own boundless generosity, the 'Fieldgate' snowdrops have become a widely-grown staple of collections everywhere and they provide a lasting legacy of a great Galanthophile.

Matt Bishop

WILLIAM R P WELCH

I am sad to report that daffodil hybridiser and grower William R P Welch, also known as Bill the Bulb Baron, died unexpectedly of cardiovascular health problems at the age of 61 over the 2019 Christmas period.

The Chinese Sacred Lily (a synonym of *N. tazetta* subsp. *lacticolor*) had been brought to California in the 19th century by Chinese immigrants and adapted quickly to its new home. As a child Bill was fascinated by this daffodil that grew in his backyard, withstood drought and seemed to thrive on neglect.

At high school Bill joined the chess club and having won several championship chess games used the prize money to start what grew to become a large collection of all the tazettas that he could get his hands on. In due course this collection became the foundation of his bulb-growing business in the Carmel Valley and subsequently Santa Cruz, California, selling cut-flowers at the local farmers' market and to flower groups and bulbs by mail order out of season.

When he started to use his tazetta collection for breeding, Bill quickly hit a problem. For many years, attractive new daffodil hybrids had successfully been bred by crossing *N. tazetta* and closely related species with other daffodils such as *N. poeticus* and *N. triandrus*. Unfortunately these hybrids are sterile and consequently had so far been

N. 'Avalanche of Gold' (*photo* **Kirby Fong**) was introduced by Bill the Bulb Baron (*photo* **Jaminia Colliard**)

an evolutionary dead end. The problem was caused by the fact that *N. tazetta* and its near relatives have a different number of chromosomes than other daffodils.

Bill overcame this problem by doubling the chromosome numbers of many sterile cultivars; thus triploids were converted to fertile hexaploids and diploids to fertile tetraploids. His target was to breed daffodils that were fragrant, vigorous, able to thrive on neglect and could be either sold as bulbs to gardeners and exhibitors or used by the cut-flower trade. So far the results have included 63 cultivars in division 8 and 5 in division 4 (doubles with one parent being a tazetta).

The American Daffodil Society Gold Medal was awarded to Bill in May 2019. The Gold Medal is awarded in 'recognition of creative work of a pre-eminent nature in the understanding and advancement of daffodils'; the citation noted his work in widening the choice of autumn cut-flower daffodils, his worldwide distribution of seeds, of which some had led to new cultivars, and the key hybridising breakthroughs that he had made.

In the United Kingdom division 8 daffodils have a relatively low profile with exhibitors and the underlying species are widely regarded as needing special care if grown outside of Cornwall. However 'Paper White' and closely related cultivars imported from Israel are sold extensively as pot plants for Christmas flowering and tazettas remain a significant crop in the Cornish cut-flower trade. Tazettas are also major commercial crops in both China and Japan and grow well in parts of the USA, Australia and New Zealand.

Bill's lifetime of work will prove to be a major legacy to all of these key commercial daffodil markets and his hobby that became a livelihood has made a big difference to the evolution of daffodils and our enjoyment of them.

Malcolm Bradbury

ADS CONVENTION AND NATIONAL SHOW 2020
11–17 MARCH 2020
Julia Hardy

After an uneventful, if not more-cleansed, flight from Dublin, I arrived in Texas to the news that the USA was closing to flights from Europe – eesh! Before departing, my husband Dave and I had joked that I might take an extended trip to see the sites of Dallas, but this was turning into no-laughing matter!

Thankfully, I was picked up from the airport and en route heard how quite a few of the convention candidates had decided last minute to cancel their travel plans. What a strange convention this was shaping up to be as news trickled through of more convention stalwarts unable to attend.

Anxious to know who, if anyone, was attending, I checked in and arrived in my room to find some very helpful daffodil fairies had sourced and filled containers for me – knowing that I'd desperately need to get my very thirsty flowers in water as they'd already been out of water well over 36 hours.

Meeting old friends was as equally pleasant as it was socially awkward in wanting to hug as usual, but awareness of social distancing was just beginning to trickle through, so we were unsure about how much physical contact we should/could have. We did get creative in greeting people now, with toe-taps, bum-bounces and elbow-bumps now the new 'hug'.

Show highlights

Thursday meant setting up my stand in a new setting using a circular table, but I was very happy with the end result, once I'd removed the flowers that didn't survive the travel and being dehydrated for so long. We also entered a few blooms for competition in the breeders' section. Amazingly, we won a few awards, which Dave and I were very happy with, including the Larus Trophy for showing our own breeding of miniature flowers (some of which were first time flowering!).

As usual the show benches were a sight to behold with many champion blooms. The epitome of all blooms were Elise Havens' 'Magic Lantern' – Best in Show; the gorgeous 'Mesa Verde' shown by Larry Force – White Ribbon for Best Vase of three blooms; and the tiny 'Pequenita' shown by Karen Cogar, which won Best Miniature.

Bob Spotts won Best Miniature seedling with one of his own breeding, a beautiful clean white multi-headed bloom, along with the Innovator award for one of his green-toned seedlings. So many awards that can all be checked out on Daffnet, along with photographs taken by the talented Tom Stettner and Kirby Fong.[1]

Elise Havens' *N.* 'Magic Lantern' won Best in Show (*all photos* **Kirby Fong**)

Bob Spotts' Seedling 3003 took the Miniature Rose Ribbon

N. 'Lemon Silk' won the Matthew Fowlds Award & Olive W Lee Trophy

Friday tour

Friday morning began with an early start for those not judging, to head to Klyde Warren Park – an interesting oasis of vegetation in Downtown Dallas. Arriving at a garden by driving underneath Woodall Rogers Freeway is not something I've ever experienced before, nor expect to again. Over two hectares (five acres), this park connects the uptown and downtown districts of Dallas – quite a feat of engineering and horticultural ingenuity.

Despite Covid 19 restrictions, Senior Vice President of Operations Michael Gaffney gave a brief history of the park and its facilities, sharing his love for the park and the fact that most of the events run on-site are free for patrons owing to very generous benefactors. The park has plans to expand by another half hectare (1.2 acres), adding a pavilion and more green space for the local residents to use.

Michael informed us about its unique biodiversity and the challenges he faces keeping plants alive in a very shallow sub-soil, surrounded by roads.

The George W Bush Presidential Library and Museum followed, which held a wealth of information on George W, his family, and his office during his administration. Who knew how much humour featured in their lives?!

Over our evening meal I caught up with friends not seen since the 2018 convention.

Saturday lectures, tour and dinner

On Saturday morning everyone could choose to join either the ADS Judges' refresher with Jack Hollister on 'Intermediates & Classics', 'Photography' with Ron Timms, or 'Heirloom gardening' with Dr William Welch and Chris Wiesinger. Yummy muffins and flavoured water kept us quenched and focused and we enjoyed gaining lots of useful information.

We were privileged to enjoy a dash around Dallas Arboretum and Botanical Gardens, which, despite closure to the public due to Covid 19, had been held open for us as a favour to the Texas Convention organiser Karla McKenzie. We saw the marvellous display put up by various individuals and groups. The grey weather made photographing the grounds a bit tricky, but I really enjoyed seeing the daffodils and tulips that seemed to be holding on to their blooms just for us.

At dinner, keynote speaker Jan Pennings lead us through his life in the Netherlands in a large family, captured in many fascinating photos; following the war and finding his own way in life, he showed us a snapshot of how he started his bulb cultivation business.

Karla gave an emotional tribute to two Dallas and ADS stalwarts – Dottie Sable (a formidable force of nature, who I felt I knew from stories regaled by Brian and Betty Duncan) and Ron Armstrong, whose son Andrew I had the honour of talking to at the Arboretum earlier. I was pleased to hear that Mitch Carney, Boonsboro, was honoured with the Silver Medal for his outstanding service to the American Daffodil Society. A few die-hard revellers were around for photo opportunities with RHS past-chair Jan and friends on this St Patrick's Day weekend.

Before we knew it we were at the 'after show' drinks party where I was regaled with stories of previous conventions and the fun had. Among this group was Michael Brook[2], who kept everyone laughing at his hilarious stories as drinks flowed until 'security' came knocking that we were being a bit too raucous! Happy memories!.

Final trips

For a slight variation to the Sunday schedule, we boarded buses to visit some stunning gardens belonging to Karla's friends and family and were then treated to food at the legendary Joe T Garcia's Mexican restaurant. We continued on to Sammy's BBQ that evening for to-die-for ribs, and a trivia quiz with daffodil-related prizes.

Sadly, with flights being cancelled, lots of delegates cut their stay short, so missed out on the trip to Mount Pleasant and Minneola on Monday when we were treated to the wonderful hospitality of Keith and Sandy Kridler, who with their son Shawn, explained how they developed their delightful space as they shuttled us around their property.

A stop-off at the brilliant Pioneer Park, where the life-size bronze statues of cattle being driven in by three mounted cowboys was quite spectacular, followed. We lunched in Annie Mae's coffee shop, a delightful little diner, before heading on to Chris Wiesinger's Southern Bulb Farm. We saw the damage that gophers can do to the bulbs and it was very interesting discussing with Chris the differences in being a British bulb farmer compared with the USA. I bought a signed copy of Chris' book, but was disappointed not to purchase some of his amazing bulbs – with no phytosanitary certificate to travel I feared they'd be confiscated.

On returning to the hotel, the landscape had completely changed with the restaurant shut completely, so the few remaining attendees had a socially-distanced last meal together, spaced around the large bar table.

I got back home the day that the airports closed to foreign travel (and Ireland began social distancing on public transport), so feel very lucky to have got to – and returned from – Texas safely, and began my 14 days quarantine before the rest of the Northern Ireland followed suit on 20 March.

Thanks go to the entire Texas team (and the ADS) for their warm hospitality through a very different convention, that we will all remember as the beginnings of a very strange time for the world as a whole. But I look forward to meeting again in happier times at future conventions and continuing to share our passion for all things daffodil!

NOTES

[1] https://daffnet.org/2020/03/2020-dallas-show-ads-national-daffodil-show-award-winners and https://daffnet.org/2020/03/2020-ads-national-convention-dallas-show-winners

[2] The Editorial Board of this publication are very sad to report that Michael Brook, daffodil exhibitor from Norfolk, has passed away due to Covid-19. Many readers may have met Mike at an ADS Convention. Our thoughts are with those he leaves behind.

AUSTRALIAN DAFFODIL SEASON 2019
Richard Perrignon

The year 2019 will go down in history as one of the worst fire seasons Australia has ever experienced. There had been a decade of drought, which I've reported year after year in these pages. It affected the daffodil season, and then the fires came soon after.

The south eastern States were engulfed by conflagration, from New South Wales to Tasmania and South Australia. Townships were destroyed; many died, including brave American aviators who helped us; the skies were red, even in Sydney; and the smoke made it difficult to breathe. Finally, the rain came – I'd thought I might never see it again – and the land was restored.

Then, in the New Year, the virus arrived with cities locked down, borders closed and the 2020 Canberra International Daffodil Convention was cancelled. By June 2020, most of the borders remained closed, but at least some of the more onerous travel and working restrictions were slowly being relaxed. In that grim series of events, daffodils provided a brief but welcome distraction. While travel was still possible, I managed, at least to get to the Canberra show.

Canberra Show *15–16 September 2019*

Stalwarts Graeme Davis, his daughter Rhiannon, Anne and Lawrence Trevanion, Andrew Carrington and Hugh Gibson were there and Helen Fleming (of Keira Bulbs fame) represented the family while Graham nursed his second knee replacement at home.

The Horticultural Society of Canberra Championship, for nine distinct stems from at least three divisions, was hotly contested. Father and son team Tony and Graeme Davis came first with an exhibit featuring cultivars largely of their own raising. Prominent among them were the Grand Champion and Champion Division 2, 'Burradoo Magic' 2W-W (pictured), with stunning flatness and poise; and a richly coloured 'Burrawang' 2Y-R of impressive proportions. Andrew Carrington came a close second. His exhibit included the Champion Division 3 and Reserve Champion: an immaculate bloom of 'Miss Rhiannon', bred by the Davis team.

In third place came Lawrence Trevanion, with the Champion trumpet – a refined pink rimmed trumpet, seedling 10/40 (1W-WWP) – and a fine example of David Jackson's celebrated all-gold double, 'Iterate' 4Y-Y (Not registered). Lawrence's dam at Yass was by

N. 'Burradoo Magic' from Tony and Graeme Davis was the Grand Champion and Champion Division 2

N. 'Affiance' exhibited by Glenbrook Bulb Farm at the Canberra Show (*all photos* **Richard Perrignon**)

this time completely dry, and most of his daffodils were only half-way out of the ground. That he managed to exhibit anything at all was a credit to him. What he lacked in quantity, he made up for in quality.

In fourth place came John Woodfield. His exhibit included the Champion Division 4, 'Muster'. John has been winning prizes with this cultivar for as long as I can remember. No one grows it like him – surely it must be his signature bloom!

Apart from the Jacksons' 'Sally Malay' 2Y-P benched by the Bruce Demonstration Garden, and a lovely bloom of Glenbrook's 'Affiance' 6Y-R (pictured), which always attracts attention, 'Iterate' was the only Tasmanian-bred flower to attract a prize. Much to my surprise, some four years or so after David Jackson's retirement, Tasmanian cultivars seem to have given way to locally-bred flowers at the Canberra show.

The Horticultural Society of Canberra Challenge, for six distinct stems from at least two divisions, went to Rhiannon Davis, daughter of Graeme. This young lady has taken over her grandmother Daphne's task of painstakingly recording all the winning entries in the show, which she does by perching her laptop computer precariously on the show benches when patrons have left. Her winning exhibit included the Champion Division 6 – an elegant bloom of Grant Mitsch's 'Rapture'. I wonder that no-one benched a bloom of Mike Temple-Smith's 'Abracadabra', which to my mind is more elegant. Perhaps it does not grow well in Canberra.

The Jacksons Daffodils Perpetual Trophy for three distinct stems from Divisions 1–4 went to Andrew Carrington, whose exhibit included another superb bloom of 'Miss Rhiannon'. In second place came B and S Hodgson, with the fiery-coloured New Zealand double, 'Kiwi Sunset'.

The Glenbrook Bulb Farm Prize for six distinct stems from Divisions 5–13, excluding miniatures, went to Team Davis, who exhibited the Champion Division 11, an

A superb Kiera Bulbs 7W-P jonquilla seedling 1/16

elegant all-yellow split-corona seedling 35/08. Keira Bulbs came second, with an exhibit that included the Champion Division 5: an elegant bicolour seedling 1-16 whose three generously deflexed florets looked like a modern candelabra. It also included a lovely bicolour 6W-Y cyclamineus seedling 1-15, and a fine bloom of Graham's own pink jonquil hybrid, 'Jocelyn Newman'. In third place came Team Davis, with a stunning 9W-GWR Poet of their own raising, which took the championships for Divisions 5–13, and for 'Other Divisions'.

The Glenbrook Bulb Farm Prize for Miniatures, six distinct, from at least three divisions, went to Lawrence Trevanion, with the tiniest bloom in the show – a single-floretted all-yellow jonquilla seedling 13/26J, not quite as big as a thumbnail, which Lawrence had picked as an afterthought. It was so small, he defied any judge to discern an imperfection. A microscope would have been needed. I tend to refer to miniatures less than 10cm (4in) high as 'ultra-miniature'. This must surely qualify as a 'nano-miniature'. Another intriguing member of Lawrence's exhibit was a triple-headed 8Y-O seedling 03/4, a small-flowered hybrid between *N. tazetta* and Section Apodanthi. Hard on his heels came Keira Bulbs in second place, with a fascinating exhibit comprising a little all-yellow jonquilla seedling 11/17 with four golden florets, a superb 7W-P jonquilla seedling 1/16 (pictured) with six florets, a rich gold example of *N. triandrus* subsp. *triandrus* var. *concolor* (Graham may well be the only Australian grower who has it), a tiny bloom of *N. hedraeanthus*, and an equally tiny all-white trumpet, seedling 17/19 which looked like its offspring.

The Canberra Gardener Championship for six vases of three stems each, one distinct cultivar per vase, from at least three divisions, went to John Woodfield, with a lovely vase of 'Bistro' 4W-O. Team Davis took both second and third places, with vases of Tony's own *N. cyclamineus* hybrid, 'Turland Gold', 'Bong Bong' 2W-W, and a beautifully proportioned all-gold *N. cyclamineus* seedling without number that I have not seen before.

Other prize winners among the standard divisions included the Hodgson's 'Kiwi Solstice', the already-mentioned bloom 'Sally Malay' from the Bruce Demonstration Garden, and a lovely intermediate *N. cyclamineus* daffodil 6W-WY bred by Keira Bulbs, unfortunately without seedling number.

Prize-winning miniatures included C Ryan and G Sheldrick's superb *N. bulbocodium* 'Wabble' 10Y-Y (not registered), bred by Lawrence Trevanion; and, despite Graham's indisposition, a number of seedlings staged by Keira Bulbs. They were a lovely yellow division 12Y-Y seedling 1–24 of unknown breeding; a tiny all-white *N. jonquilla* seedling 1–19 bred from *N. dubius*; a tiny yellow *N. cyclamineus* seedling 75g-19, two all-yellow *N. triandrus* seedlings with lots of florets in Graham's inimitable style, a lovely all-yellow *N. jonquilla* seedling 58–19, and some beautiful bicolor 6W-Y *N. cyclamineus* seedlings 1C-19 and 1A-19.

Though definitely not daffodils, having regard to the bulb-oriented nature of this journal it would be remiss of me not to mention the stunning displays of potted *Pterosytylis*, which always seem to distinguish this show – Australian bulbous terrestrial orchids whose appearance is reminiscent

of fritillaries: this time, *P. curta*, *P. baptistii* and *P. ralpheraenai*.

Tasmania 2019

I am grateful to Mary Crowe of the Tasmanian Daffodil Council for being my 'eyes and ears' in Tasmania. Mary writes: "2019 saw an extended daffodil season in Tasmania. A warmer July followed by a colder August/September meant that many flowers bloomed early, while mid and late season flowers were available for a longer period than usual.

The show season began at Claremont where a wonderful display of blooms was presented principally by Glenbrook Bulb Farm, Janelle and Jon Noble and Owen Davies. It promises well for the future that Owen is benching some beautiful seedlings and his seedling 15/98 ('Crucial Point' × 'Lutana') 2W-O won Grand Champion Daffodil. Janelle and Jon Noble had some fine seedlings and match it with the enthusiasm of the young.

Helen Blowfield won a few champion blooms at Hobart with Jackson Daffodil flowers, 'Uncensored' being particularly favoured at a number of shows. In the North of the state Jackson Daffodils were prominent, while David Pyke displayed some excellent seedlings, often using locally raised daffodils such as 'Pink Belladonna' and 'Lady Diana' (not registered).

Miniature daffodils were well represented at all shows, Kevin Crowe winning Best Miniature at Hobart, Claremont and All Saints shows - all three exhibits were different 6W-W seedlings. In the North, Sam Biggins benched winning miniatures of Glenbrook breeding. In Launceston, it was pleasing to see Noel Button, a fairly new exhibitor, win Best Miniature with 'Angel's Whisper'."

It is very pleasing that younger breeders are doing well at Claremont, and one hopes that daffodil shows elsewhere in Australia might attract such exhibitors. With any luck, the borders will open again in 2021 and we may all be able to meet again at an International Daffodil Convention, hopefully in Australia.

NEW ZEALAND DAFFODIL SEASON 2019
Denise McQuarrie

Fewer frosts than usual and good winter rainfall meant an early daffodil season for the North Island, with blooms of excellent quality for most regions. An especially early and condensed season for the Waikato left few daffodils in bloom by the end of September. In the lower half of the South Island the season was a little later than usual with plenty of good blooms still open well into October.

North Island Show
14–15 September 2019

Gisborne, on the east coast of the North Island, was the venue for the North Island Show on 14–15 September. Exhibitors know that the hospitality shown by members of the Poverty Bay Horticultural Society is legendary and well worth the long journey to get there. There were 1,800 blooms exhibited, down on last year, but it was still a very good show.

Fisher Nurseries won Class 1, the Rhodes Cup, for twelve New Zealand raised cultivars, three blooms of each with their usual large smooth flowers –'Cosmic Ice' 1W-W and 'Jamore' were their best vases. Aaron Russ, making the journey from Christchurch, won the NDS Raisers Challenge Cup from two other good entries. Aaron included three of his outstanding 1W-Y varieties in the collection. One of these, seedling AR54-01B was selected as the 1W-Y Premier Bloom. Miller Daffodils in second place included their lovely split-corona 'Jean Estelle' 11aW-YWP, and in third place Graham Phillip's entry included his very colourful 4W-P seedling U97-1.

Class 5, the George Yarrall Trophy for twelve cultivars, one bloom of each, was also won by Fisher Nurseries; a brilliantly coloured 'Oak Ridge' 2W-P caught the eye. 'Cosmic Ice', which they grow to perfection, the 1W-W Premier Bloom came from this entry.

The David Adams Medal Class calls for twelve distinct daffodils from at least six divisions. The winners, Malroze from Canterbury, included a miniature 'Ninepins' 3W-YOO, an Intermediate seedling MOP19-1 and the 2W-W Premier Bloom MCQ-OC16 in their entry. The Daffodil Society Gilt Medal was won by Fisher Nurseries who exhibited some cultivars not seen at New Zealand shows before, including 'Benjamin' and 'Barbara Ann', both of which impressed; they should be very useful additions for exhibitors when more widely grown. Aaron Russ did very well in the Collection classes and included many of his own seedlings in his winning entries.

The number of entries in the Open Single Bloom classes were down, with the class for 3W-O/R/P being best supported with twelve. It was won by Mike Smith with 'Polar Gift' 3W-YYO. John Hollever took the 2Y-Y class of eleven entries with a lovely bloom of the smooth and reliable 'Sandmere Gold' and won the Most Points prize in the Single Blooms.

Entries in the Miniature Section were up on last year. This section is always popular with the public; indeed it was hard to get a close look on the Saturday afternoon. Malroze took the Miniature Daffodil Championship with the colourful 'Ninepins' 3W-YOO featuring in their entry. Of note too were the many other attractive seedlings throughout this section both from Malroze and other raisers.

The Intermediate section, with an expanded schedule, has gone from strength to strength, but, with Intermediate enthusiast Wayne Hughes absent because of ill health, entries were down from last year. Denise McQuarrie won the Intermediate Championship for six blooms of named cultivars and 'Tayforth Small One' 2Y-O was selected as Best Intermediate in Show.

The Amateur section was keenly contested. The Avery Challenge Trophy for nine cultivars, three blooms of each had two entries with Lisa and Raymond Watkins the winners; their best vase being 'Wayby' 2Y-R. Robin Simmons in second place included a good vase of the 1Y-Y 'Kinghorn' in his entry. Lisa and Raymond headed off two other entries to win the Waikato Trophy for twelve blooms with an

Champion Bloom in show at the NDS North Island Show went to *N.* 'Luminosity' grown by Mike Smith (*photo* Trevor Rollinson)

excellent entry; 'Cameo Magic' 4W-W and 'Copper Sheen' 2O-R being their best flowers. Trevor Rollinson with his usual neat, well-staged daffodils won the George Parr Trophy for six blooms. The Don Bramley Trophy for six New Zealand Raised blooms had six entries and was won by Brian Mackenzie's outstanding entry that included 'Cape Farewell' 4W-WYR, a red-pink double bred by John Hunter.

The Premier Blooms were well spread among exhibitors. Amateur Champion Bloom was an excellent 'Wayby' grown by Lisa and Raymond Watkins. Champion Bloom in show was a beautiful bloom of the well-named 'Luminosity' 2YYW-W (pictured) grown by Mike Smith, a first-time Champion Bloom for him. Congratulations Mike, I'm sure it will be the first of many.

Reserve Champion was a 'Trena' of great form exhibited by Malroze. I noted a very elegant Clive Postles' seedling 294 1W-Y, which was Best British Raised Bloom for Fisher Nurseries – it surely has a great future on the show bench.

First Class Certificate

At this show the NDS Floral Panel awarded a First Class Certificate as an exhibition flower to 'Ameeya', 4W-W. This outstanding double, raised by the late Peter Ramsay, was put forward for the well-deserved award by his wife Lesley.

Altogether it was a most enjoyable weekend for those attending. Thank you to the Poverty Bay Horticultural Society and especially NDS members Gill Coates and Anne Pole and the team for being such great hosts.

South Island Show

28–29 September 2019

A fortnight later exhibitors headed to Timaru in South Canterbury for the South Island Show on 28–29 September. The Timaru Horticultural Society was celebrating its 150th jubilee and this show was part of the celebrations. It was a big show with 2,411 entries, more entries than the World Convention Show at Dunedin in 2012.

Aaron Russ won the Rhodes Challenge Cup for twelve New Zealand raised cultivars, three blooms of each, his entry consisting of mostly his own bred flowers, including several good pinks and an excellent vase of seedling AR68-01A, a 3Y-W. John Hunter repeated his success of last year by winning the NDS Raisers Cup for twelve blooms It was good to see many of John's latest registrations in his entry, including his excellent 2W-Ps 'Emotion' and 'Forever'.

Bill Cowie won the British Raisers Cup for nine cultivars, three blooms of each. He included good vases of 'Clouded Yellow' and 'Honeybourne'. Class 4 The Oamaru Cup for three cultivars, three blooms of each from three divisions had a special prize linked to it. This was the Old Mates' Memorial Prize in remembrance of friends Neil McQuarrie and Kevin Kerr who both passed away during the year after battling cancer. There were eight entries with Malroze winning with a lovely set. 'Fleeting Glimpse' 2Y-YYR with its longish rimmed cup stood out in their entry.

The International Trophy for twelve cultivars was won by Denise McQuarrie from three other entries. This entry was rather depleted after Premier Bloom selection as it had five Premier blooms chosen from it; seedling MCQ-M13, 3W-YYR with its sharply defined rim stood out. 'Bramcote Gem' an elegant 1W-Y was also very good, here and elsewhere in the show.

The nine bloom classes had excellent entries; even the 1Y-Y class had five entries, which is surprising so late in the season. The David Bell Trophy for three blooms each of three division 11 cultivars had eight good entries with John Hollever heading off Mike Smith. Both included 'Trigonometry', which has become a standard in this division. Mike also included seven of his own seedlings in his entry.

The Single Bloom classes had good entries with the largest class for 3W-O/R having 17. Denise McQuarrie won it with a good bloom of 'Greenhill Rata' 3W-YYR. The Ramsay Pink Trophy for one registered pink was won by Mike Smith with an impressive 'Cape Point'.

Entries in the Miniature Section were well up with 205 stems. Malroze won the Miniature Daffodil Championship for nine cultivars. They included 'Ninepins', 'Effigy' 2W-O and 'Kakariki' 3W-O all bred from *N. atlanticus* crossed with a Poet seedling. They added a welcome dash of colour to the miniature section. Another bloom of 'Kakariki' (pictured) was later selected as Best Miniature in show.

The Intermediate entries were well up with 122 blooms shown. The Pleasant Valley Daffodil Trophy for six named varieties was won by Denise McQuarrie with 'Pinto Pony' 2W-O and 'Georgie Pie' 2YYW-W both being selected for Premier Blooms. The 2Y class had eight entries and was won by Fisher Nurseries with an excellent bloom of 'Reg Nicholl', a very desirable little flower. Best Intermediate in show was a 4W-P seedling MCQ-H2B.

Entries also rose in the Amateur Section. Lisa and Raymond Watkins of Waikato won the

N. 'Kakariki' was selected as Best Miniature in show at the NDS South Island Show (*photo* **Malcolm Wheeler**)

South Island Daffodil Championship for three blooms each of nine cultivars. 'Everytime' 2Y-R and popular 'Kiwi Happy Prince' 2W-YYR added great colour to their collection.

The Alfred Clark Trophy for twelve cultivars was hotly contested with six excellent entries. Greg Inwood won from Trevor Rollinson and Garfield and Bev Andrew in a very tight contest with Premier Amateur Large-Cup 'Archie Boy' 2Y-O being selected from Greg's entry.

There was a large number of Amateur Multi-bloom entries with Phil and Lynne Wild from South Canterbury doing very well and winning the Most Points prize. The Single Bloom Section was also well supported with some classes having twelve entries. Jack Inwood won the Most Points Prize. In the Novice Section it was great to see new members Neil and Judy Judd from Dunedin doing splendidly at their first show.

The Premier Blooms were of a high standard. The Best British Raised bloom was a very good 'Altun Ha' exhibited by Aaron Russ. The stem of 'Delltone' 7Y-O from John Hollever was outstanding.

N. 'Kowhai Glen' – raised and exhibited by Denise McQuarrie – took Champion Bloom of show at the NDS South Island Show (*photo* **Megan McQuarrie**)

Champion Amateur Bloom was an excellent 'Crowndale' exhibited by Arch Crerar. It was rather a field day for Denise McQuarrie who was awarded 18 Premier Blooms including the Reserve Champion, a very full and symmetrical stem of 'Harpswell' 8W-Y with 18 florets. Raised by the master of Tazetta breeding, Wilfred Hall, 'Harpswell' is proving to be an excellent show variety. Champion Bloom of Show, a large and impressive 'Kowhai Glen' 2Y-Y (pictured) was also exhibited by Denise and was one of her own raising.

It was a pleasure to attend the show and thanks go to the hosts for a great weekend.

At present are living in uncertain times with the challenges we face due to Covid-19 and it is still not known how this coming season will unfold. Let us hope that the world will return to some form of normality soon.

WAKEFIELD AND NORTH OF ENGLAND TULIP SOCIETY SHOW IN SWEDEN 2020
James Akers

The Wakefield and North of England Tulip Society (WNETS) is the oldest society holding tulip shows in the United Kingdom. The Society in any correspondence always adds 'established in 1836' however it is older than that – the society was actually formed in 1807[1] when, as the Wakefield Florists' Society, it held its first exhibition at the Grand Stand, Outwood, Wakefield on Monday 27 April 1807. This show was for auriculas, but pinks, carnations, dahlias and tulips soon followed; daffodils were not considered a florists' flower. The earliest tulip show for the Society that has been found reported on in local newspapers was held on 1 June 1829, but as the report begins 'This Society held their Annual Show of Tulips...' we can be sure it wasn't the first. What is certain is that until 2019 a show was held every year including each year of the two World Wars. Copies of most of the reports can

be found on the Society website[2]. But then came 2020 and, despite attempts to maintain this continuity, Government Regulations prevented it.

However, all was not lost. For several years the Society had maintained close contact with a number of tulip enthusiasts in Sweden, with an interchange of visits, and several bringing flowers from Sweden to Wakefield for the Annual Show. Eventually Tulip Group – en sidolök till Wakefield and North of England Tulip Society was formed. Google translates 'sidolök' as onion but the Swedish language does not distinguish between onion and bulb, I'm reliably informed. A 'sidolök' is the term for a young bulb that appears next to the main bulb; in other words an 'offset'.

A get-together had already been arranged in Sweden, for the week after the Annual Show in England, and because restrictions in Sweden allowed outside gatherings, this was expanded to include a small Show of just five classes including the class for the Gina Roozen Cup, awarded for three breeders. No-one from the

ABOVE: Exhibitors waiting for the staging call at the hastily organised Wakefield and North of England Tulip Society Annual Show, Halmstad Corona version 2020, in Sweden;

BELOW: Judge Ulf Hansson and assistant Josef Wellfelt in action (*all photos* **Marit Eriksson**)

United Kingdom was able to attend but a visual/audio link enabled those members to see the event for several hours. Because I am unable to comment on individual flowers or exhibits, having not seen them in the flesh, I will just list the winning entries and the main awards at the Wakefield and North of England Tulip Society Annual Show, Halmstad Corona version 2020, held in the garden at Neptunigatan 38, Halmstad, Sweden, Lördag (Saturday) 16 Maj 2020.

Winners

Three Stages Breeder, Flame and Feather one bloom of each
1st Morgan & Marit Eriksson: 'James Akers', 'Lord Stanley' and 'Sir Joseph Paxton'
One Breeder
1st Emilie Wellfelt: 'Wendy Akers'
One Flame
1st Emilie Wellfelt: 'Wakefield'

One Feather
1st Niklas & Katrin Wellfelt: 'James Wild'
Gina Roozen cup Three discrete Breeders
1st Emilie Wellfelt: 'Mabel', 'James Akers', 'Trefoil Guild'
Best Breeder in show: Morgan & Marit Eriksson – 'James Akers'
Best Flame in show: Emilie Wellfelt – 'Wakefield'
Best Feather in show: Niklas & Katrin Wellfelt – 'James Wild'

I am grateful to Emilie Wellfelt and Ulf Hansson for their help in providing information for this show.

NOTES

[1] http://wnets.org.uk/the-search-for-the-societys-origin/?LMCL=sNV4PR
[2] http://wnets.org.uk/show-reports-pre-1907

Reprinted from the Daily Telegraph 25 March 2020 with the permission of Telegraph Media Group Limited.

UK shows

The worldwide Covid-19 pandemic led to lockdown being imposed by law in the United Kingdom on 23 March 2020. As a result all flower shows due to be held after that date were cancelled. Consequently we are unable to publish many of the reports that we would normally have included, but are pleased to be able to share details of those that took place prior to lockdown:

AGS SHOWS 2020
Robert Rolfe

The Alpine Garden Society held just five shows during February and March before, in common with other organisations countrywide, it was obliged to cancel its remaining programme of events. Of those that took place, I wasn't able to attend the final one in Kendal (neither did many others, for by then alarm was widespread). It was also lucky that I was able to make it to the first two, held

G. *plicatus* 'Trym seedling' exhibited by Bob and Rannveig Wallis at AGS South Wales Show (*all photos* **Jon Evans**)

in South Wales and at Pershore, because widespread flooding almost cut off the approach roads, with the Severn at Worcester having overflowed its banks and caused flooding as far as the eye could see, while on the motorways, aquaplaning made being given a lift in a sports utility vehicle (SUV) a relief.

The enduringly mild weather of the previous few months, dating back to Christmastime (in Sutherland, 18.7C/65.7F was recorded, Britain's highest maximum temperature for that time of year), saw many snowdrops at their best several weeks early. Indeed, easily the best display brought indoors that I witnessed was at an AGS West Yorkshire Group meeting as early as 11 January, when Anne Wright (more of whom later) staged a non-competitive grouping based on her Dryad Gold Group raisings, dating from 2006 (they first flowered four years later).

These deliberate crosses with the parentage G. *plicatus* × *nivalis* (= G. × *valentinei*) have collectively several attributes, viz. their stems stand resolutely upright rather than splay, they exhibit marked variations on a theme, and by and large, they have proven vigorous. The earliest, G. × *valentinei* 'Dryad Gold Sovereign', was eclipsed by a spectacular clump of (this time round) contemporaneous G. × *valentinei* 'Dryad Gold Bullion', at 8cm (3.15in) tall, around half the height of some other selections. It has the further advantage of increasing well. 'Why is there never a show on the day you need one?', their raiser reflected.

South Wales Show, Caerleon
15 February 2020

A surprisingly abundant gathering, given the adverse conditions (it rained in torrents from start to finish, and the event was closed early on this account). Three of the four small six-pans included at least one snowdrop, the most eye-catching of them the show secretaries' G. *plicatus* 'Trym seedling' (Bob & Rannveig Wallis) (pictured), an as-yet unchristened addition to the inverse poculiform range that already numbers clones named for their

N. 'Snow Baby' exhibited by Lesley Travis won the Tomlinson Tankard at the Pershore Early Show

offspring and grandchildren such as 'Corrin'.

This said, overall snowdrops had peaked a couple of weeks previously, and pickings were relatively thin, though with distinguished exceptions, notably Bob Worsley's G. 'Peg Sharples', meticulously top-dressed with Cambark (backdrops of pebbles and grit are inferior and unsympathetic) that was awarded the Galanthus Goblet.

First brought to attention in the early 1970s, this is an EB Anderson derived seedling from its Cumbrian namesake, with a typically late-flowering proclivity.

Staying on the west side of the country, G. 'Compton seedling no. 3' (Diane Clement) was one of several Margaret Owen snowdrops that this exhibitor brought to attention over the course of several shows. Meanwhile, in the Novice Section, Anita Acton's G. *lagodechianus* helped her win the Caerleon Cup (for most first prize points therein) and was the best of its kind seen in several years.

Show secretaries Bob & Rannveig provided numerous entries and two of the most memorable were their slightly bicoloured *N. alpestris* × *N. cyclamineus*, in a very small pot, full of flower (this 2003 seedling now takes the unregistered clonal name 'Noddy') and a creamy yellow *N. romieuxii*, flowering a month or more later than its accustomed December/January typical timing.

Pershore Early Show *22 February 2020*

A well-attended, creditable gathering, where miniature daffodils and snowdrops were present in some numbers, the majority of them familiar rather than novel. One such, Lesley Travis's *N.* 'Snow Baby' (syn. 'Ice Baby') (pictured), helped her gain the Tomlinson Tankard (most first prize points in the Intermediate Section).

She was challenged by Anita Acton, who had a convincing win in the three-pan bulbous plants class with *Galanthus* 'David Shackleton',

G. 'Little Ben' shown by Diane Clement at Pershore

G. 'Cicely Hall' and G. 'Annette'.

Now kicked upstairs and obliged to do battle in the Open Section, Ben & Paddy Parmee submitted G. 'Kildare', G. 'E. A. Bowles' and G. *nivalis* 'Tiny Tim'. Mike Morton's *Narcissus fernandesii* was the best of some six entries in various classes, junior and senior.

The Henry Hammer Cup for most first prize points in the Novice Section was claimed by Henry Fletcher, his entries including a fetching *N. cyclamineus*, neither drawn nor overfed (unlike other examples on show!) and demonstrating why, when at its best, this moisture-loving Galician is peerless.

Early Spring Show 29 February 2020

A change of venue, for the first time held at Theydon Bois, Essex, on a day that witnessed everything from bright sunshine to heavy sleet. In truth not an event that, this year at least, brought together a rich gathering of *Amaryllidaceae*, and of those that appeared,

there were some hiccups. These included Andrew Ward's *Narcissus* 'Whippet' (a first outing for Anne Wright's raising *N. rupicola* × *N. cyclamineus*, unfortunately declared NAS in the absence of any notes in its class). More happily, local exhibitor Maurice Bacon's accomplished *N. henriquesii* secured him the George Smith Salver for the best pan of bulbs in the Novice & Intermediate Sections.

Those representatives that chiefly adorned the Open Section have already been covered in previous reports, notable among them Mike Chadwick's *N. triandrus* 'Isabella' (not registered), *Galanthus* 'Little Ben' (pictured) from Diane Clement (she also entered a good clump of G. 'Compton seedling no. 2'), a well-established *N. alpestris* courtesy of Bob & Rannveig Wallis, and *N.* 'Bowles's Early Sulphur' × *N. cyclamineus* 'Sweet Sue' (not registered), a Blackthorn raising shown by far-travelled Alan Newton.

Readers' knowledge will be put to the test

Ben and Paddy Parmee's artfully arranged miscellanies of showdrops, miniature daffodils and other spring blooms allowed exhibitors to showcase fairly new acquisitions

by the artfully arranged, multifaceted blend of miniature daffodils and snowdrop cultivars (pictured) conjured up by Ben and Paddy Parmee. These beautiful assemblages afford visitors the opportunity to compare and contrast these delicate new offerings at very close quarters – and let exhibitors showcase fairly new acquisitions they haven't had time to build up into serviceable show clumps.

Loughborough Show *7 March 2020*
The Parmees entered a further inspired, similarly duo-genus focused flower arrangement a week later, equally well-composed (despite the long journey from Hampshire) yet involving a substantially different cast. They also vied with other exhibitors in the pot plant classes, where an overall first-rate medley of dwarf bulbs,

along with veteran examples of dionysias, *Porophyllum saxifrage* hybrids, various *Corydalis* and *Primula allionii* clones was the centrepiece of the display. Such eclectic mixes are a hallmark of this show, only a year shy of its 30th anniversary. Exhibitors countrywide tirelessly, annually bring this about.

That said, I started by mentioning Anne Wright's non-competitive offerings at an AGS Local Group meeting in January, and will end by focusing exclusively on the plants she brought (in three plastic bakers' trays, loaded to the hilt) that truly galvanised the day's representation of miniature *Narcissus*. A substantial number had never before been exhibited at this show, reprising her early endeavours with home-raised *N.* 'Jim Lad' (*N. rupicola* × *N. asturiensis* 2Y-Y) and *N.* 'Sidora' (*N. cyclamineus* × *N. asturiensis* 1Y-Y)

At the Loughborough Show, this multitudinous 'Minionette' from Anne Wright took the Royal Bank of Scotland Trophy for best pan of bulbs. It also received a Preliminary Certificate and Cultural Certificate

in the later 1980s, first acclaimed at this event in 2001. Much has changed since, not least ongoing hybridisation programmes, her cross-influence on Brian Duncan, and imports of inspired hybrids from Tasmanian Glenbrook Bulb Farm (Rod Barwick) and Canberra-based Keira Bulbs (Graham and Helen Fleming). The results achieved and the inventiveness implicit have, in a very few years, been transformative.

She had nine entries, some of them three-pans, five receiving first prizes, all the others placed. I start by saluting her multitudinous N. 'Minionette' [1] (pictured): just 12cm (4.7in) tall and with flowers to 42mm (1.65in) wide, greenish-yellow and with ribbed coronas, originally distributed under the number AW2674 and representing N. rupicola subsp. marvieri × N. cyclamineus 6Y-Y (registered in 2018), recipient of the Royal

Bank of Scotland Trophy for the best pan of bulbs. The flowers have female-influenced short coronas and pronouncedly reflexed perianth segments. Avid filmgoers will recognise the reference to 'Despicable Me'.

A couple of parent stocks, Alec Gray's N. 'Candlepower' 1W-W and Keira's creamy N. cyclamineus seedling N. 'Second Fiddle' 6W-W, have proved especially productive. Part of a three-pan entry, perky N. rupicola × 'Second Fiddle' AW2990-2 is now registered as 'Sweet Petite' (two seedlings were raised, inseparable). It is just 7-8cm (2.75-3.15in) tall, greenish-white with a slightly deeper-coloured, scented 12mm (4.7in) long corona, the leaves ascending, narrow and neatly ordered. N. 'Dormouse' (N. rupicola 'Spring Charm' × 'Second Fiddle' 1 W-Y) (pictured) is equally diminutive and equally fragrant, with

117

Diminutive and fragrant 'Dormouse' was also shown by Anne Wright at Loughborough

slightly smaller, pale greenish-ivory, short-trumpeted flowers on 8cm (3.15in) stems.

N. 'Little Dryad' (N. 'Candlepower' × KB/M/1/98) references Anne's Tockwith nursery, ivory-cream but with a longer trumpet and emphatically reflexed petals, while seedling AW3762-17 ('Snipe' × 'Candlepower') is also of clear merit but unregistered at the time of writing.

For good measure, also Glenbrook, Australasian N. 'Coo' was the only monocot accorded a Certificate of Merit (one of six; two or three times the usual ration).

Mentioned in despatches: N. 'Mitimoto' 10W-Y with rich citric trumpets and almost white perianth segments, from Tasmania (Glenbrook), dating from the late 1980s, and the surprisingly late-flowering elegant N. obesus × N. cantabricus var. petunioides seedling AW4216. Another name is in the offing.

Finally, in the last decade or so, Anne has also transferred her skills to snowdrop breeding – often utilising the chipping technique Brian Duncan describes in the 2018 Yearbook (pp32–35): some resolutely refuse to make up by any other means. I'll finish with her virescent G. nivalis AW3856, two very similar seedlings so far not named, but valuable additions to the ever-increasing range of these heavily green-marked dignitaries.

NOTES

[1] At the show, the Joint Rock Garden Plant Committee gave a Preliminary Certificate and a Cultural Certificate to N. 'Minionette' 6Y-Y (pictured) and a Preliminary Certificate to N. rupicola × 'Second Fiddle' subject to it being given a cultivar name, both awards to flowers shown by Anne Wright. No other awards to daffodils, snowdrops or tulips were made during the spring season 2020.

NORTHERN IRELAND DAFFODIL GROUP WINTER SHOW 2020
Richard McCaw

It was good to return to Colemans Garden Centre, Templepatrick for the Northern Ireland Daffodil Group (NIDG) Winter Show on 29 February 2020. Colemans is situated about 32 km (20 miles) from Belfast and had recently undergone a multi-million-pound refurbishment. Around 18m (60ft) of table space was set up in the heart of the garden centre, early on the Saturday morning and we could have used more. Many visitors at this popular venue were encouraged to become more interested in the blooms on display.

We welcomed exhibitors from all of Ireland and England, not forgetting Yorkshire! With almost £300 of prize vouchers, success was hard to come by and competition very strong. There were about 250 daffodils, miniatures and standards and 125 snowdrops on display. Plus, well-filled classes for crocus, hellebores, foliage, bulbous and non-bulbous plants. Little did we know that this show was to be the only one in 2020 in association with NIDG, because of Covid-19, so it's ironic that this was the best Winter Show the NIDG has held.

In Class 1 for three named Miniature Daffodils bred by exhibitor, two Titans of the miniature world clashed. Brian Duncan the victor with 'Fantine' 6W-Y, Best Miniature Narcissus and Best Exhibit in show, 'Pet Lamb' 1W-W and 'Cheeky Chappie' 6W-Y. Anne Wright was a close runner-up with 'Fresh Breeze' 6Y-Y, 'Deryn' 5W-Y and 'Mica' 2W-W.

It's always good to see what breeders are bringing on. Class 2, for Unregistered Miniature seedlings, had the same placing with three beautiful flowers from both. Brian's were 3031 6W-W, 4367 12Y-Y and 3234 6W-Y and Anne's 2949-1-17 6Y-WWY, 3110-1-16 1Y-Y and 4259-1-18 1Y-Y.

Class 4, the Championship class for six stems, was won by Anne Wright, featuring three seedlings plus 'Palomino' 6W-Y, 'Mica' and 'Little Dryad' 6W-W. 'Candlepower' 1W-W and 'Punk' 1Y-Y were Dave Hardy's best in his second-placed entry. Chris Bone was third; best here was 'Gipsy Queen' 1YYW-WWY.

'Roundita' 1Y-Y won the Three Blooms Division 1, in another well-filled class, shown by Dave Hardy. Three Blooms Division 6, was won by Brian Duncan with 'Fling' 6W-W. A nice vase of 'Tiny Bubbles' 12Y-Y shown by Chris Bone won the class for Three Blooms Any Other Division.

In the Single Bloom classes, 'Starlit' 1W-W shown by Maurice Kerr won Division 1.

Derrick Turbitt took first and second in the Division 6 class with a very nice seedling 6W-W (*N. cyclamineus* × 1W-W sdg). Chris Bone's 'Little Becky' topped the Any Other Division class.

A pot, any size, any number of blooms, was won by Derrick Turbitt with another beautiful seedling, 'Small Talk' × *N. cyclamineus* 6Y-Y.

Best bloom in the Intermediate (max 80mm) Section was a seedling by Nial Watson 332 11aY-O. Best Standard Daffodil was 'Causeway Gem' 6Y-Y for Derrick Turbitt.

In the *Galanthus* section Anne Wright took Best Exhibit with *G. alpinus* var. *alpinus* (pictured). Other blooms and exhibits of note were 'Green Mile', shown by B McCandless and a lovely yellow snowdrop, *G.* 'Wendy's Gold'.

Best Bulbous Plants exhibit was taken by Brian Duncan for a fine pot of yellow *Crocus*.

By the time Richard Fry MD of Colemans Garden centre stepped up to present the major prizes a large crowd had gathered and Richard offered his thanks to all.

In any other year this tremendous show would have been a fantastic curtain raiser to our Daffodil season. Alas not to be and our dreams can only be carried on to 2021.

Galanthus alpinus var. *alpinus* took best exhibit in the Galanthus section for Anne Wright at the NIDG Winter Show (*photo* Anne Wright)

Brian Duncan's *N.* 'Fantine' won best Miniature Narcissus and Best Exhibit in show (*photo* Brian Duncan)

RHS shows and competitions

RHS ROSEMOOR DAFFODIL AND HYACINTH COMPETITIONS 2020
Jackie Petherbridge

Despite cases of Covid-19 beginning to emerge in Devon and Cornwall, this was a splendid show. It seems to have a special place in people's hearts and, with support from National Trust gardeners and other great estate gardens in the southwest of England, camellias, magnolias, rhododendrons of all kinds were magnificent this year – together with some splendid bulb entries.

Daffodil collection and single-bloom classes

About 120 named cultivars, plus seedlings, graced the show benches. A superb effort considering that this is such an early spring shows with some regular exhibitors absent.

The Crystal Trophy class for six cultivars of standard daffodils made a real impact with five competitive entries. Richard Gillings won the class with a nicely balanced and beautifully presented set of flowers both old and new. These included 'I Love You', an early 2W-W show winner that made its debut here at Rosemoor as a seedling, 'Queen's Guard' and an old favourite 'Park Springs'. His yellow perianth selections were 'Golden Choice', 'Corby Candle' and another southwest favourite 'Cape Cornwall' (pictured). Zara Evans was second with 'Habit', 'Engagement Ring', 'Corby Candle', 'Golden Choice', 'Beaulieu' and 'Snowboard'. 'Golden Choice' was also included in Ivor Clark's third-placed entry along with 'Ombersley', 'Shockwave', 'Arleston', 'Flammea' and 'Online'.

Ivor Clark had some lovely blooms in the Division 1 and 2 classes but couldn't quite match those of Richard Gillings. Nevertheless, second out of 15 entries in the Division 1 Y-Y blooms class and second in the Division 2 class with 13 entries is no mean feat. His winning form also showed in a fine set of 'Pink Silk' and 'Tangerine Dream'. Richard meanwhile exhibited 'Habit' to winning effect and his 'Cape Cornwall' was Best Bloom in show.

Doubles were excellent this year and there were nine entries in their single bloom class. Richard Gillings came first with a good-sized, well-layered, symmetrical bloom of reliable 'Heamoor'. John Gibson's second placed 4Y-O seedling 298-4-03 is certainly one to watch and the results could have been reversed if the judging taken place later, in a warmer hall.

Divisions 5-8 and 11 are always well supported at this show and their grace and elegance are a great favourite among visitors.

'Ice Wings', 'Surfside', 'Trena' and 'Avalanche' were worthy winners for show regular Marie Bersey. Peter Wilkins exhibited a really nice set of 'Harmony Bells' and 'Perky'. 'Rapture' displayed its winning form for Zara Evans. 'Maria Pia' with its good colour and form was Division 11 cultivar of choice for Zara Evans, Peter Wilkins and John Gibson.

There are some unusual competitive classes at Rosemoor. I particularly like the all-comers vases where competitors can exhibit leftover blooms or just group flowers together in a vase for decorative effect. Not always easy to judge, sometimes your heart is tempted to overrule your head, but they do make a pleasing display and a break from the discipline of competitive single or multi bloom vases. Local competitors Frances Howard, Marie Bersey and National Trust Killerton had an eclectic mix of good quality flowers but John Gibson's vase was judged to be the best for diversity and effect.

Intermediate daffodils were in short supply but John Gibson's seedling 522 7 05 with yellow orange-flushed petals had a lovely form. As indeed did John's many miniature entries. John won the Nine Miniature Cultivars, Species or Wild Hybrids class in

Nine Miniature Cultivars, Species or Wild Hybrids from John Gibson (*all photos* **Michael Baxter**)

2019 and repeated his success, albeit with many of his closest competitors absent this year. All his entries were seedlings, many of his own raising, and each one beautifully presented including the convention of alternating petal colours up and down the nine-bloom exhibit (pictured). A lovely trumpet on the yellow 201-31-15 compensated for the unconventional twisted petals yet the whole effect on a miniature bloom was proportioned and delightful. The differences between flowers emerging from identical crosses proved a talking point with visitors and judges as did the size and form of flowers achieved by crossing *N. obesus* with 'Mitimoto'.

More success for John came from a delicate arrangement of *N. cyclamineus, N. graellsii* and *N. bulbocodium*. However, Zara Evans was hot on his heels with some super miniature exhibits. Her Division 6 'Hummingbird' was judged Best Miniature exhibit in the show and, maybe not the freshest, but still well formed and proportioned, were her flowers of 'Alec Gray'. Colin Street found success with 'Angel's Whisper' and 'Golden Ring'.

I love to see the larger forms of species and wild hybrids exhibited and Tansy Parsons

picked up first place with three charming blooms of *N. moschatus* that just pipped John Gibson's entry of *N. hispanicus*. Another feature of this show is a wealth of historic daffodils. National Trust Killerton's first-place vase contained 'Twink', 'Minnie Hume', 'Cynosure', 'Firebrand' and 'Gloria Mundi'. Frances Howard had some splendid 'Empress' as did Edwin Lanyon with 'Seagull'. Edwin also showed 'Ozan', a cultivar I'd not seen before and came first in the pre-1940s class with aptly-named white/orange 'Sunrise'.

Frances Howard's second place entry was all-yellow double 'Great Leap' and, being a pre-1940 cultivar, the form did indeed show an advance with more fullness and layering. Adrian Scamp, as always, had an exceptional display of daffodils including many charming 'historics' thus ensuring that these blooms remain in cultivation. Blooms from all Divisions 1 to 13 were represented on his trade stand and presentation was superb, as always. A precursor for his customary gold medal display at RHS Cardiff, it feels unjust that the quality of this exhibit cannot be recognised with a medal, especially as Cardiff and all future shows were cancelled this year.[1]

N. 'Cape Cornwall'

Pot classes

For a masterclass in pot growing, look no further than Peter Wilkins' winning examples. A superbly-grown pot of 'Pacific Coast', a multi-headed miniature in peak condition with strong stems, staked and correctly dressed with grit. Ditto 'Jimmy Noone', a large bright colourful trumpet with good foliage, again superbly presented. We missed, alas, the spectacle of the alpine bulb entries and the wonderful range of potted bulbs Carlos van der Veek usually brings from the Netherlands.

Hyacinth competition

Few people grow and show hyacinths better than John and Jean Gibson and size, richness of colour and immaculate presentation are their trademarks. Peter Wilkins had some creditable entries but the Gibsons swept the board. Perhaps the most striking and skilful entries are those with multi blooms and the colour and form of the winning seven cultivars in growth in a bowl was exquisite. The multi-coloured sight and sensation of 'Frankie', 'Blue Jacket', 'Aiolos', 'Snowblush', 'Goluboj Elektron', 'Queen of the Violets' and 'Yellowstone' was a real encouragement for this bulb to be more widely grown.

NOTES

[1] The RHS Bulb Committee did not make any awards to daffodils, hyacinths or tulips during the spring season 2020.

RHS Rosemoor Daffodil Competition 2020
Results compiled by Peter Wilkins

1 Six cultivars, one bloom of each, any division or divisions. (5) 1 R Gillings: Golden Choice, Park Springs, I Love You, Cape Cornwall, Corby Candle, Queen's Guard; 2 Mrs Z Evans: Habit, Engagement Ring, Corby Candle, Golden Choice, Beaulieu, Snowboard; 3 I Clark: Golden Choice, Ombersley, Shockwave, Arleston, Flammea, Online.

2 Three cultivars, three blooms of each, any division or divisions. (1) 1 I Clark: Corby Candle, Pink Silk, Ombersley.

3 Division 1, one bloom. (15) 1 R Gillings: Habit; 2 R Gillings: Gold Velvet; 3 I Clark: Golden Choice.

4 Division 1, three blooms, any cultivar or cultivars, in one vase. (6) 1 R Gillings: Habit; 2 I Clark: Golden Choice, Ombersley x2; 3 P F Wilkins: Jimmy Noone.

5 Division 2, one bloom. (13) 1 R Gillings: Cape Cornwall (Best Bloom in Show); 2 I Clark: I Love You; 3 R Gillings: Tropical Heat.

6 Division 2, three blooms, one or more cultivars, in one vase. (7) 1 Mrs T Parsons: I Love You; 2 I Clark: Shockwave; 3 P F Wilkins: Cape Cornwall, Impeccable x2.

7 Division 3, one bloom. (3) 1 I Clark: Tangerine Dream; 2 P F Wilkins: Nice Day; 3 C Down: Sunrise.

8 Division 4, one bloom. (9) 1 R Gillings: Heamoor; 2 J Gibson: 298-4-03; 3 Mrs Z Evans: Heamoor.

9 Division 5, one bloom. (6) 1 Mrs M Bersey: Ice Wings; 2 P F Wilkins: Harmony Bells; 3 Mrs M Bersey: Thalia.

10 Division 6, perianth yellow, corona white or coloured, one bloom. (6) 1 Mrs Z Evans: Rapture; 2 R Gillings: Warbler; 3 Mrs M Bersey: The Alliance.

11 Division 6, perianth white, corona white or coloured, one bloom. (4) 1 Mrs M Bersey: Surfside; 2 P F Wilkins: Perky; 3 Mrs M Bersey: Trena.

12 Division 6, three blooms, any cultivar or cultivars, in one vase. (3) 1 Mrs M Bersey: Trena; 2 Mrs Z Evans: Rapture; 3 P F Wilkins: Perky.

13 Division 11, one bloom. (7) 1 Mrs Z Evans: Maria Pia; 2 P F Wilkins: Maria Pia; 3 J Gibson: Maria Pia.

14 Any other division, one bloom. (7) 1 C Down: *N. poeticus* Ornatus; 2 P F Wilkins: Avalanche; 3 Mrs M Bersey: Nickelodeon.

15 Any other division or divisions, excluding division 13, three blooms, one or more cultivars. (3) 1 Mrs M Bersey: Avalanche; 2 P F Wilkins: Falconette; 3 E Lanyon: Royal Connection.

16 Five blooms from divisions 1 to 4 and 11, excluding miniatures, one or more cultivars, in one vase. (4) 1 Mrs Z Evans: Beaulieu, Corby Candle, Proud Fellow, Habit, Heamoor; 2 I Clark: Chobe River x2, Pink Silk, Queen's Guard, Golden Choice; 3 Mrs M Bersey: Gallipoli Dawn, Seedling, Banker, Unknown x2.

17 Five blooms from divisions 5 to 10, excluding miniatures, one or more cultivars, in one vase. (3) 1 Dr F Howard: Thalia, Skype, Sweetness, Avalanche, Pride of Cornwall; 2 Mrs M Bersey: Rapture, Sidhe, Thalia, Orange Comet, Trena; 3 P F Wilkins: Avalanche x2, Falconette, Rapture x2.

18 Five blooms from any division or divisions, one or more cultivars/species, in one vase. (2) 1 Mrs M Bersey: Diversity, Thalia x2, Cool Evening, Trigonometry; 2 C Down: Bath's Flame, Avalanche, Lucifer, Minnie Hume, Unknown.

19 One vase of daffodils to be judged for diversity and decorative effect. (2) 1 J Gibson: Multiple blooms not recorded; 2 Dr F Howard: Multiple blooms not recorded

20 Intermediate cultivar from divisions 1 to 4 and 11, one bloom. (1) 1 J Gibson: 522-7-05.

21 Miniature species or wild hybrid from division 13, excluding bulbocodiums, one bloom single headed. (0)

22 Miniature species or wild hybrid from division 13, excluding bulbocodiums, one bloom multi headed. (3) 1 J Gibson: *N. intermedius*; 2 Mrs Z Evans: *N. tazetta. aureus*; 3 Mrs T Parsons: *N. fernandesii*.

23 One miniature cultivar, excluding division 10, one bloom single headed. (2) 1 Mrs Z Evans: Hummingbird (Best Miniature in Show); 2 J Gibson: 623-26-10.

24 One miniature cultivar, excluding division 10, one bloom multi-headed. (2) 1 C Street: Angel's Whisper; 2 C Street: Baby Boomer.

25 One bulbocodium, either from division 13 or division 10, one bloom. (5) 1 J Gibson: G 501 (*N. obesus* x Minimoto); 2 Mrs Z Evans: Mary Poppins; 3 E Lanyon: Oxford Gold.

26 Three miniature blooms from division 1, one or more cultivars, in one vase. (1) 1 Mrs Z Evans: Alec Gray.

27 Three miniature blooms from division 6, perianth yellow, one or more cultivars, in one vase. (0)

28 Three miniature blooms from division 6, perianth white, one or more cultivars, in one vase. (0)

29 Three miniature species, one bloom of each, in one vase. (1) 1 J Gibson: *N. cyclamineus, N. graellsii, N. bulbocodium*.

30 Three miniature cultivars, excluding division 10, one bloom of each, in one vase. (2) 1 Mrs Z Evans: Little Becky, Alec Gray, Hummingbird; 2 J Gibson: G 195 M, 623-26-10, Zeekic.

31 Three blooms of bulbocodiums from divisions10 and/or 13, one or more cultivars/species. (2) 1 C Street: Golden Rings; 2 Mrs Z Evans: Oxford Gold.

32 Nine miniature cultivars, species or wild hybrids, any division or divisions, one bloom of each. (1) 1 J Gibson: 702-32-12, G 613, 201-31-15, G 616-49-10, 623-26-10, G 623, G 501 (*N. obesus* x Minimoto), G 821 (*N. obesus* x Minimoto).

33 One species or wild hybrid from division 13, excluding miniatures, 3 blooms in one vase. (2) 1 Mrs T Parsons: *N. moschatus*; 2 J Gibson: *N. hispanicus*.

34 A pot or pan of miniature hybrid daffodils. (1) 1 P F Wilkins: Pacific Coast.

35 A pot or pan of miniature species daffodils. (0)

36 A pot or pan of non-miniature daffodils. (1) 1 P F Wilkins: Jimmy Noone.

37 Five blooms of historical daffodils, registered pre-1940, any division(s), one or more cultivars. (3) 1 C Down: Twink, Mini Hume, Cynosure, Firebrand, Gloria Mundi; 2 Dr F Howard: Empress x5; 3 E Lanyon: Seagull x5.

38 Three blooms of historical daffodils, registered pre-1940, any division(s), one or more cultivars. (3) 1 E Lanyon: Ozan; 2 Dr F Howard: Thalia; 3 C Down: Irene Copeland, Bath's Flame, Lucifer.

39 One historical daffodil cultivar, registered pre-1940, 1 bloom. (15) 1 E Lanyon: Sunrise; 2 Dr F Howard: Great Leap; 3 C Down: Gloria Mundi.

40 A pot or pan of any bulbs other than daffodils or hyacinths. (0)

41 Alpine bulbs, a collection of; 3 pots or pans, any species or cultivars. (0)

RHS Rosemoor Hyacinth Competition 2020

Results compiled by Peter Wilkins

1 Three cultivars, three blooms of each, single florets, each cultivar displayed in one pot or pan. (1) 1 J & J Gibson: Queen of the Pinks, Yellowstone, Indigo King.

2 Three cultivars, one blooms of each, any colour(s), in one pot or pan. (0)

3 One cultivar, three blooms, single florets, in one pot or pan. (3) 1 J & J Gibson: Blue Jacket; 2 P F Wilkins: Pink Surprise; 3 J & J Gibson: Aiolos.

4 One cultivar, one bloom, single florets, any colour, in one pot or pan. (3) 1 J & J Gibson: Queen of the Violets; 2 J & J Gibson: Blue Jacket; 3 P F Wilkins: Pink Surprise

5 One cultivar, one bloom, double florets, any colour, in one pot or pan. (1) 1 J & J Gibson: Pink Royal.

6 A pot or pan of hyacinths. (1) 1 J & J Gibson: Frankie, Blue Jacket, Aiolos, Snowblush, Goluboj Elektron, Queen of the Violets, Yellowstone.

Plant index

Tulipa

lehmanniana 78
lemmersii 82
Lilliput 78
linifolia **77**
London 86
Lord Stanley 112
luanica 83
Mabel 112
Maureen **90**,91,92
Menton 90,91,92,93
Mrs. John T. Scheepers 91
narcissicum 83
neustruevae 78
Olympic Flame 91
Orange Princess 91
orphanidea 77,79

orthopoda 77
ostrowskiana 78,79
Oxford **86**
Pieter d'Leur 91
Pink Impression 91
polychrome 78
Prinses Irene 85,**86**
Purissima 91
Red Gem 77
Red Hunter 77
regelii 84
Renown 92
Roosevelt 86
saxatilis 79
Sir Joseph Paxton 112
sprengeri **76**,77,85

Spring Green 91
sylvestris 76,79
talassica 82
tarda 76,77
Toyota 90,91,**92**,93
turgaica 83
turkestanica 77
urumiensis 77
Vivex 90,91,92,**93**
Wakefield 112
Wendy Akers 112
World Peace 91
World's Favourite 90,91,93
zenaidae 78
Zomerschoon **85**
zonneveldii 84

RHS Bulb Committee 2020

Chairman
Mrs T Clements

Vice Chairmen
Mr SJ Gibson
Mr A Street

Members
Mr JJ Amand
Mr M Bishop
Mr C Blom
Mr MS Bradbury
Dr J David
Mr JGM Davies
Mr R Evans
Mrs J Hardy
Mr R Hyde

Mr R McCaw
Mr JS Pennings
Mrs JM Petherbridge
Mr A Shipp
Lady Skelmersdale, VMH
Dr N Sterling, CBE
Mr C van der Veek
Mr JW Walkers
Mr NA Watson
Mr RA Wilford
Mr P Wilkins
Mrs A Wright

Honorary Members
Mr JW Blanchard, VMH
Mr BS Duncan, MBE
Mr R Nicholl

Mr RAD Scamp

Corresponding Members
Mr J Almond
Mrs J Currie
Mrs S Exley
Mr LP Olive
Mr N Porteus
Mr MA Vandervliet
Mr N Wray

Friends of the Committee
Mr JL Akers, MBE
Dr PE Brandham

* Secretary
Mr M Pitcher

RHS Narcissus Classification Advisory Group 2020

Chairman
Mr NA Watson

Vice Chairman
Mr BS Duncan, MBE

Members
Mr MS Bradbury
Mr E Breed
Mr CD Brickell, CBE, VMH
Mr SJ Gibson
Mrs ML Gripshover
 (also National Registrar)

Mrs S Kington
Mr R Nicholl
Mr RAD Scamp
Lady Skelmersdale, VMH
Mr C van der Veek

National Registrars
Mr GC Davis (Australia)
Mrs ML Gripshover (USA)
Mr W Hall (New Zealand)
Drs J van Scheepen
 (The Netherlands)

Honorary Member
Mr JW Blanchard, VMH

Corresponding members
Mr JL Akers, MBE
Mrs D McQuarrie
Ms S Van Beck

Ex officio
Dr J David

* Secretary
Mrs M Underwood